JONATHAN EDWARDS ON PRAYER

31 BIBLICAL INSIGHTS TO DEEPEN AND ENRICH YOUR PRAYER LIFE.

GODLIPRESS TEAM

© **Copyright 2022 by GodliPress. All rights reserved.**

This book is copyright protected. You cannot amend, distribute, sell, use, quote or paraphrase any part, or the content within this book, without the consent of the author or publisher, except in the case of brief quotations embodied in critical articles or reviews.

Scripture quotations are from The ESV® Bible (The Holy Bible, English Standard Version®), copyright © 2001 by Crossway, a publishing ministry of Good News Publishers. Used by permission. All rights reserved

CONTENTS

Introduction	vii
1. WHY DOES GOD LISTEN TO US?	1
A God of Grace	1
A Mediator of Mercy	2
Daily Reflections	4
2. PRAY WITHOUT CEASING	5
Daily Reflections	7
3. WHY MUST WE ASK FOR BLESSINGS?	9
Daily Reflections	11
4. PRAYING FOR FORGIVENESS	13
Daily Reflections	15
5. PRAYING FOR GOD'S GLORY	16
Daily Reflections	19
6. GOD HEARS US	20
God Gives Us Access	20
God Is Ready to Hear	22
Daily Reflections	23
7. GOD ANSWERS US	24
God Answers Abundantly	24
God Is Moved by Prayer	26
Daily Reflections	27
8. WHY WE MUST PERSEVERE IN PRAYER	28
Daily Reflections	30
9. NEGLECTING PERSONAL PRAYER	32
Daily Reflections	34
10. IDOLS CANNOT HEAR YOUR PRAYERS	36
Daily Reflections	39

11. WHY PEOPLE STOP PRAYING   40
Daily Reflections   43

12. GRACE TO PRAY   45
Daily Reflections   47

13. SEEKING GOD IN PRAYER   49
Daily Reflections   51

14. CAN CHILDREN PRAY IN MEETINGS?   53
Daily Reflections   55

15. REASONS HYPOCRITES DO NOT PRAY   57
Daily Reflections   61

16. A CRY GOD WILL NOT HEAR   62
Daily Reflections   64

17. THE PRAYER OF PSALM 139   66
Daily Reflections   69

18. PRAYER IS HOLY   70
Daily Reflections   73

19. PRAYING AGAINST TEMPTATION   75
Daily Reflections   77

20. REVIVAL PRAYER   79
Daily Reflections   82

21. UNITY IN REVIVAL PRAYER   83
Who Will Come Pray?   83
How Will They Come?   84
Daily Reflections   85

22. SECRET PRAYER   87
Daily Reflections   90

23. PRAYING FOR THE LOST AS JESUS DID   91
Daily Reflections   94

24. EMOTIONAL PRAYER   95
Daily Reflections   97

25. PRAYING FOR GOD'S WILL IN SUFFERING   99
Daily Reflections   102

26. PRAYING FOR IMPORTANT BLESSINGS 103
Daily Reflections 106

27. PRAYERS OF THE SAINTS 108
Why Does God Honor Our Prayers? 109
Daily Reflections 110

28. IRREVERENCE IN PRAYER 112
Daily Reflections 115

29. JESUS, OUR MEDIATOR 116
Daily Reflections 118

30. JESUS' PRAYER FOR THE HOLY SPIRIT
TO COME 120
Daily Reflections 122

31. AN EXAMPLE TO WATCH AND PRAY 124
Daily Reflections 127

About Jonathan Edwards 129
Bibliography 133

INTRODUCTION

There are many books in Christian bookshops unpacking every topic imaginable, and many of these are thick volumes on how and when to pray. But a large portion of modern books focuses on techniques and quick fixes rather than the real aspect of what prayer is and its importance in our lives. There is something about the writers of old that still rings true, above all the glossy self-help guides. There is a biblical truth that we see in the example of Jesus' life.

Jonathan Edwards spent much of his time as a pastor laying foundations, outlining the church's position on issues, and defending the gospel. Many people disputed the correct manner of the sacraments, arguing over doctrinal issues while the state of their hearts was not in line with God.

There is a tone in much of his writing that comes across as direct and even argumentative for this very reason. His most famous sermon, *Sinners in the Hands of an Angry God,* is as

viii | *Introduction*

straightforward and uncomfortable as they come and is often perceived as a hard pill to swallow.

But in reality, Edwards was soft-spoken, hardly ever raising his voice from the pulpit, and he was methodically encouraging. Instead of reading his words as a cold rebuke, if we see them as exhortations for us to live right and pray right so that one day we will be with Jesus in heaven, then we can see his heart behind the message.

His scientific mind and logical approach to each issue are backed up by the Bible every time. It is this clear, scriptural outline that makes Edwards' work so easy to read but sometimes difficult to digest because there is no hiding from the challenge that he lays out before us. This challenge is a call for us to realign our prayer lives with the gospel.

To avoid losing any of the meaning or emphasis while bringing Edwards' words into a more modern format, care has been taken to preserve and present them as though you were reading the original. Passages and excerpts have been thoughtfully selected to bring you the best of his work in today's language.

In a book that can easily be read over a month, this 31-day guide is perfect for gleaning the precious perceptions and treasures that Edwards offered over 200 years ago. The message is still as powerful today as it was then. Daily reflections have been added to assist in bringing a deeper reflection of the text in regard to your own prayer life.

Making these classic writings on prayer accessible to a wider audience of Christians means that many more people will be

Introduction | *ix*

able to benefit from these timeless insights. We can all continue to grow in our prayer lives to bring us another step or two closer in our relationship with the Lord. We all need to pray because, "He that lives a prayerless life, lives without God in the world."

1

WHY DOES GOD LISTEN TO US?

"But truly God has listened;
he has attended to the voice of my prayer"
Psalm 66:19

A God of Grace

First, because he is a God of infinite grace and mercy. It is incredible that God should be so ready to hear our prayers, even though we are so despicable and unworthy. That he should give us free access at all times, should allow us to be persistent without seeing it as arrogance, and should be so rich in mercy to us that call on him—that worms of the dust should have such power with God by prayer, that he should do such great things in answer to our prayers, and should show himself to be moved by them.

This is incredible when we think of the distance between God and us, how we have provoked him by our sins, and how unworthy we are of the least gracious notice. It cannot be from any need that God has in us, because there is nothing good in us. Neither can it be from anything in us to turn the heart of God to us. It cannot be of any worth in our prayers, which are polluted things. But it is because God delights in mercy and reaching down to us. This is what distinguishes him from all other gods. He is the great fountain of all good, from whom goodness flows as light from the sun.

A Mediator of Mercy

Second, we have a glorious Mediator, who has prepared the way, that our prayers may be heard consistently with the honor of God's justice and majesty. Not only has God sufficient mercy for this, but the Mediator has provided that this mercy may be exercised consistently with divine honor. Through him, we can come to God for mercy. He is the way, the truth, and the life. No man can come to the Father but by him. This Mediator has done three things to make way for our prayers to be heard.

1. By his blood, he has made atonement for sin, so that our guilt does not need to stand in the way, as a separating wall between God and us, and that our sins might not be a cloud that our prayers cannot pass through. By his atonement, he has opened the way to the throne of grace. God would have been infinitely gracious if there had been no Mediator, but the way to the mercy seat would have been blocked.

But Jesus has removed whatever stood in the way. The veil which was before the mercy seat *"was torn in two, from top to bottom"* (Matt. 27:51) by the death of Christ. If it had not been for this, our guilt would have remained as a wall of brass to stop our approach. But it is all removed by his blood (Heb. 10:17).

2. Jesus, by his obedience, has purchased this privilege —that the prayers of those who believe in him should be heard. He has not only removed the obstacles to our prayers but has merited a hearing of them. His merits are the incense offered with the prayers of Christians, which makes them a sweet fragrance to God, and acceptable in his sight. So, the prayers of Christians have power with God: At the prayer of a poor worm of the dust, God stopped the sun for a whole day. Jacob had power with God and succeeded. Our prayers would be nothing and disregarded by God if it were not for the merits of Jesus.

3. Jesus enforces the prayers of his people by his intercession at the right hand of God in heaven. He has entered into the holy of holies for us, with the incense which he has provided, and there he makes continual intercession for everyone who comes to God in his name, so that their prayers come to God the Father through his hands. *"And another angel came and stood at the altar with a golden censer, and he was given much incense to offer with the prayers of all the saints on the golden altar before the throne, and the smoke of the incense, with the prayers of the saints, rose before God from the hand*

of the angel" (Rev. 8:3-4). This was shown by the priest's offering incense in the temple, at the time when the people were offering up their prayers to God. *"And the whole multitude of the people were praying outside at the hour of incense"* (Luke 1:10).

Daily Reflections

Have you ever wondered why God would bother listening to us, especially considering how sinful and worthless we are? Yet he does. Despite what we deserve, he bends his ear and listens, waiting to pour out his love on us. It is one of the mysteries of grace that God would even give us the time of day, let alone send his only son to die for our sins so that we might be reconciled.

1. Why does God listen to you?
2. What does grace mean? Look at Romans 3:24.
3. What did Jesus' sacrifice on the cross do for us? How does this impact our prayers?
4. Why do we have the privilege of praying to God?
5. How does Jesus intercede for us as a High Priest?

2

PRAY WITHOUT CEASING

"Pray without ceasing"
1 Thessalonians 5:17

To motivate you to continue in prayer, think about how much you always need God's help. If we stop praying, it means we do not need his help any further, that we have no reason to go to God with requests and supplications. But, in reality, it is in God we live, move, and have our being.

We cannot take a breath without his help. You need his help every day for the supply of your physical needs, and especially to help your souls. Without his protection, we would immediately fall into the hands of the devil, who always stands as a roaring lion, ready to devour us when he gets the chance. If God preserved your lives but left you to yourselves, you would be very miserable—your lives would be a curse to you. Those who are born again, if God should forsake them, would soon fall away from grace into a more miserable place than before they were born again. They have no strength of their own to resist those powerful enemies who surround them. Sin and Satan would immediately carry them away like a mighty flood if God should forsake them.

You stand in need of daily supplies from God. Without God, you can receive no spiritual light or comfort, can exercise no grace, can bear no fruit. Without God, your souls will wither and die away, and sink into a terrible state. You continually need the instructions and directions of God. What can a little child do in a desert without someone to guide it and lead it in the right way? Without God, you will soon fall into traps, pits, and a terrible end. Since you are in continual need of God's help, you should continually seek it from him, and acknowledge your dependence on him by bringing your needs before him and offering up your requests to him in prayer. How miserable we would be if we stopped praying, and God stopped taking care of us.

Being constant in prayer does not profit God, and if we stop, God will sustain no damage—He does not need our prayers. But if God stops caring for us and helping us, we immediately sink—we can do nothing and can receive nothing without him.

Carrying on in prayer is one of the best ways to make your soul flourish and prosper. It is an excellent way of keeping up a relationship with God and growing in the knowledge of God. It is the way to a life of communion with God. It is an excellent way of keeping the heart away from the pleasures of the world and causing the mind to focus on heaven. It is an excellent preservative from sin and a powerful antidote against the devil's plans. Prayer gives strength from God against the lusts and corruptions of the heart and the world.

Prayer keeps the soul alert and guides us to walk with God. It brings us to be fruitful in good works in keeping with the doctrine of Christ and makes our light shine before others, that they, seeing our good works, shall glorify our Father in heaven. And, if we are constant in prayer, it will be enjoyable. Laziness is what makes it such a burden for some people.

The power prayer has with God causes us to become like Jacob, who succeeded when he wrestled with God for the blessing. See the power of prayer represented in James 5:16-18: "*Therefore, confess your sins to one another and pray for one another, that you may be healed. The prayer of a righteous person has great power as it is working. Elijah was a man with a nature like ours, and he prayed fervently that it might not rain, and for three years and six months it did not rain on the earth. Then he prayed again, and heaven gave rain, and the earth bore its fruit.*"

Daily Reflections

To pray continually seems impossible. We need to stop and do our work, perform our daily duties, and we need to sleep. And yet, the Bible is very clear that we should not stop praying. If we can understand this in the spirit, that it is not a physical requirement or command, then we will find that it is more possible than our natural minds imagine. To be in an attitude of prayer is not something that comes easily or

8 | JONATHAN EDWARDS ON PRAYER

quickly, but it is learned over time and with the help of the Spirit.

1. Why is realizing we need God's help such good motivation to help us continue in prayer?
2. Why is carrying on in prayer one of the best ways to make your soul flourish and prosper?
3. It seems a strange statement that Edwards makes about God not benefiting from our prayers. Do you agree with this?
4. Do you find it difficult to continue in prayer during the day when there are so many distractions and demands?
5. What makes prayer become such a burden for us?

3

WHY MUST WE ASK FOR BLESSINGS?

"Ask, and it will be given to you"
Matthew 7:7

Why does God need us to ask for blessings he knows we need? It is not because he must be informed of our needs or desires. He is omniscient, and with respect to his knowledge, unchangeable. God never gains any knowledge by information. He knows what we want a thousand times better than we do ourselves before we ask him. Even though God is sometimes represented as if he were moved and persuaded by the prayers of his people, he is not. For it is not possible that there can be any new inclination or will in God. The blessing of God is not moved by anything in us.

The spring of God's generosity is within himself. He is self-moved, and whatever blessing he gives, the reason for it is not found in us but in God's own good pleasure. It is the will of God to give blessings in this way: in answer to prayer when he plans beforehand to give them when he has promised them. *"I am the Lord; I have spoken, and I will do it. Thus says the Lord God: This also I will let the house of Israel ask me to do for them"* (Eze. 36:36-37).

God has given prayer to be the method for asking for blessings. And he is pleased to give blessings in consequence of prayer, as though he were moved by prayer. When the people of God are stirred up to prayer, it is the effect of his intention to show mercy. Therefore, he pours out the spirit of grace and supplication.

There may be two reasons why God requires prayer in order to give blessings: one is about God, and the other is about ourselves.

1. With respect to God, prayer is a sensible acknowledgment of our dependence on him for his glory. As he has made all things for his own glory, so he will be glorified and acknowledged by his creation. And it is right that he should require this from those who are the subjects of his mercy, that when we want to receive any blessing from him, we should humbly supplicate the Divine Being. Giving that blessing is just an acknowledgment of our dependence on the power and mercy of God for that which we need, and the honor that should be paid to the great Author and Fountain of all good.

2. With respect to ourselves, God requires prayer of us in order to give blessings, because it tends to prepare us for receiving them. Sincere and passionate prayer tends to prepare the heart. Our sense of need is heightened, and the value of that which we seek, as well as our desire for it, so that the mind is more prepared to enjoy and respect it, to rejoice in it when received, and to be thankful for it. Prayer, with the right confession of words, can highlight a sense of our unworthiness of the blessing we seek. By placing ourselves in the immediate presence of God, it can make us aware of his majesty, and in a sense, fit to receive blessings from him. Our prayer to God may fill us with realizing our dependence on God for the blessing we ask, and to have faith in God's sufficiency, so that we may be prepared to glorify his name when the blessing is received.

Daily Reflections

Thinking that God knows everything far before it has happened or before it is spoken is often too much for our human brains to comprehend. When it comes to prayer, many of us have asked a similar question: Why do we need to ask when God already knows what we need or what we are about to say? Regardless of his omniscience, he still wants us to ask.

1. Read Psalm 139:4. What do you understand by this verse?

2. Do you think it is alright just to pray in our minds since he knows our thoughts, or do we need to actually say the words?
3. Read 1 John 1:9. How does this relate to the previous question?
4. Why do you think God enjoys prayer even when it does not benefit him?
5. What are the two reasons why God requires prayer from us?

4

PRAYING FOR FORGIVENESS

"For your name's sake, O LORD, pardon my guilt, for it is great"
Psalm 25:11

It is evident in this psalm that when it was written, it was a time of hardship and danger for David. This is clear from verse 15 onward: *"My eyes are ever toward the LORD, for he will pluck my feet out of the net."* His distress makes him think of his sins and leads him to confess them and cry to God for forgiveness. *"Remember not the sins of my youth or my transgressions;" "Consider my affliction and my trouble, and forgive all my sins"* (Psalm 25:7, 18).

We can see in the psalm what arguments he makes use of in asking for forgiveness.

1. He pleads for pardon for God's name's sake. He has no expectation of forgiveness for any of his own righteousness or worthiness, for any good deeds he had done, or any compensation he had made for his sins. Though if a person's righteousness could be used as a plea with God, David would have had as much to plead as most. But he begs that God would do it for his own name's sake, for his own glory, for the glory of his own free grace, and for the honor of his own faithfulness to his covenant.

2. David uses the greatness of his sins as an argument for mercy. He does not plead his own righteousness or the smallness of his sins; he does not say, "Forgive my iniquity, for I have done a lot of good to counterbalance it"; or, "Forgive my iniquity, for it is small, and you have no real reason to be angry with me; my sin is not so great that you have any reason to remember it against me; my offense is enough to be overlooked."

But instead, he says, "Forgive my iniquity, for it is great": He pleads the size of his sin, and not the smallness of it; he enforces his prayer with how bad his sins are. But how could he make this a plea for forgiveness? Because the greater his iniquity was, the more he needed forgiveness. It is as if he had said, "Forgive my iniquity, for it is so great that I cannot bear the punishment; my sin is so great that I am in need of pardon; my case will be exceedingly miserable unless you are pleased to pardon me." He makes use of the greatness of his sin to enforce his plea for pardon, as a person would make use of the greatness of hardship in begging for relief.

When a beggar begs for bread, he will plead the greatness of his poverty and necessity. When a man in distress cries for pity, what better plea can be used than the extremity of his case?—And God allows such a plea as this: For he is moved to mercy toward us by nothing in us but the miserableness of our case. He does not pity sinners because they are worthy, but because they need his pity.

Daily Reflections

Forgiveness is an area that many Christians struggle with. Failure to be able to forgive, or not knowing how to forgive properly, often leaves many believers stranded. It is not easy, especially when we feel so deeply that we have been wronged in some way. But here, the spotlight is not on us forgiving others, but rather on us needing to be forgiven. If we can come to this place, see our need for it, and ask for forgiveness, we will find we have more grace to be able to pardon others.

1. Do you find it easy to ask God for forgiveness? Why?
2. Why do you think David found it necessary to use arguments to plead for forgiveness?
3. Why is God's name's sake a powerful argument when asking for anything?
4. Why is God moved by David's plea that highlights the magnitude of his sins?
5. Why do you think pleading and begging are important aspects of this type of prayer?

5

PRAYING FOR GOD'S GLORY

"Not to us, O LORD, not to us, but to your name give glory"
Psalm 115:1

The glory of God is spoken of as consisting and having the value of certain virtues.

- Faith: *"No unbelief made him waver concerning the promise of God, but he grew strong in his faith as he gave glory to God"* (Rom. 4:20). *"Every tongue confess that Jesus Christ is Lord, to the glory of God the Father"* (Phil. 2:11).
- Repentance: *"My son, give glory to the LORD God of Israel and give praise to him. And tell me now what you have done; do not hide it from me"* (Josh. 7:19).

- Kindness: *"This act of grace that is being ministered by us, for the glory of the Lord himself and to show our good will"* (2 Cor. 8:19).
- Thanksgiving and praise: *"Was no one found to return and give praise to God except this foreigner?"* (Luke 17:18). *"The one who offers thanksgiving as his sacrifice glorifies me; to one who orders his way rightly I will show the salvation of God!"* (Psalm 50:23).

The goal of Christianity is to glorify God. In the Old Testament, they thought they did this by offering many sacrifices, but God corrects their mistake and tells them that it is not attained this way, but by offering the more spiritual sacrifices of praise and prayer.

In the Bible, we see that we should desire and seek God's glory as our highest and last goal in what we do. *"So, whether you eat or drink, or whatever you do, do all to the glory of God"* (1 Cor. 10:31). *"That in everything God may be glorified"* (1 Peter 4:11).

Jesus requires his followers to desire and seek God's glory above all things else, which we see from that prayer he gave his disciples as the pattern and rule: *"Hallowed be your name"* (Matt. 6:9). This is the same language about glorifying God as we see in Leviticus 10:3, Ezek. 28:22, and many other places. Our last and highest goal should be our first desire, and consequently first in our prayers. So, we can argue that Jesus shows us that God's glory should be first in our prayers. Therefore, we can argue that since Jesus shows us that God's glory should be first in our prayers, this is our end goal.

This is further confirmed by the conclusion of the Lord's prayer, *"For thine is the kingdom, and the power, and the glory"* (Matt. 6:13 KJV). In connection with the rest of the prayer, it implies that we desire and ask for all the things mentioned in each petition, with submission to the dominion and glory of God; in which all our desires ultimately are fulfilled, as their end goal. God's glory and dominion are the two first things mentioned in the prayer, and are the subject of the first half of the prayer; and they are the two last things mentioned in the same prayer, in its conclusion. God's glory is the Alpha and Omega in the prayer. From this, we can argue that God's glory is the end goal of creation.

The same thing, Jesus seeking the glory of God as his ultimate end, is shown by what he says at the time of his final suffering in that remarkable prayer, the last he ever made with his disciples on the evening before his crucifixion. In it, he expresses the sum of his aims and desires. His first words are *"Father, the hour has come; glorify your Son that the Son may glorify you"* (John 17:1). As this is his first request, we can assume it to be his supreme request and desire, and what he ultimately aimed at in everything. If we consider what follows to the end, all the rest that is said in the prayer seems to be but an amplification of this great request. It is clear that Jesus Christ sought the glory of God as his highest and last end; and that this was God's end goal in the creation of the world.

Daily Reflections

Giving God glory should be our ultimate goal in everything we do. Making this one of our constant prayers in every personal prayer time we have focuses us on God's will. We can see that even Jesus did this, as he spoke often about it and prayed that he might fulfill this in his life on earth. To have such an example leaves very little argument that we should have the same goal in our Christianity if we want to please God.

1. What does God's glory mean to you?
2. Why is it the main and end goal of Christianity? Read Isaiah 43:7 to see how we fit into this.
3. Why are the sacrifices of praise and prayer worth more than animal sacrifices?
4. How do we go about glorifying God in everything that we do? Is it possible to do this?
5. How do we go about praying for the glory of God?

6

GOD HEARS US

"O you who hear prayer"
Psalm 65:2

God Gives Us Access

In his Word, he shows he will always allow us this privilege. He sits on a throne of grace, and there is no veil to hide this throne and keep us from it. The veil is torn from the top to the bottom. The way is open at all times, and we may go to God as often as we please.

Although God is infinitely above us, we can come with boldness. *"Let us therefore come boldly unto the throne of grace, that we may obtain mercy, and find grace to help in time of need"* (Heb. 4:16, KJV). How wonderful that worms like us should be allowed to come boldly at all times to such a great God—he indulges all kinds of people, of all nations. *"All those who in every place call upon the name of our Lord Jesus Christ, both their Lord and ours: Grace to you"* (1 Cor. 1:2-3).

God allows the most wicked and unworthy: The greatest sinners are allowed to come through Jesus. And he not only allows but encourages and frequently invites them, showing that he delights in being sought by prayer. *"The prayer of the upright is acceptable to him"* (Prov. 15:8). And in Song of Songs 2:14, we have Jesus saying to the bride, *"Let me hear your voice, for your voice is sweet."* The voice of Christians in prayer is sweet to Jesus, and he delights to hear it.

He allows us to be sincere and persistent to the point of not accepting denial, to give him no rest, and even encouraging us to do so. *"They shall never be silent. You who put the LORD in remembrance, take no rest, and give him no rest"* (Isa. 62:6-7). So Jesus encourages us in the parable of the persistent widow and the unjust judge (Luke 18), and in the parable of the man who went to his friend at midnight (Luke 11:5).

God allowed Jacob to wrestle with him, to be determined: *"I will not let you go unless you bless me"* (Gen. 32:26). It is a good thing when people are violent for the kingdom of heaven and take it by force. So, Jesus left the blind man to become very persistent in his cries to him. He continued crying, *"Son of David, have mercy on me!"* (Luke 18:39). Others who were there rebuked him and told him to be quiet, seeing it as arrogant behavior toward Jesus to call out to him as he passed by. Jesus did not rebuke him but stood and commanded that he be brought to him, saying, *"What do you want me to do for you?"* (Luke 18:41). And when the blind man told him, Jesus graciously granted his request.

The freedom of access that God gives is seen in allowing us to come to him by prayer for everything we need, both physical and spiritual, whatever evil we need to be delivered from, or good we want to obtain. *"Do not be anxious about anything, but in everything by prayer and supplication with thanksgiving let your requests be made known to God"* (Phil. 4:6).

God Is Ready to Hear

He often shows his readiness to hear prayer by answering quickly, sometimes while we are still speaking, and sometimes before we pray when we have only thought of praying. So ready is God to hear prayer, that he takes notice of the first purpose of praying, and sometimes blesses us because of it. *"Before they call I will answer; while they are yet speaking I will hear"* (Isa. 65:24). We read that when Daniel was making supplication, God sent an angel to comfort and assure him of an answer (Dan. 9:20-24). When God decides to delay his answer to the prayer of faith, it is not because he does not want to answer, but sometimes for the good of his people, that they may be better prepared for the blessing when they receive it, or because another time would be the best.

And even then, when God seems to delay an answer, the answer is quick, as in Luke 18:7-8: *"And will not God give justice to his elect, who cry to him day and night? Will he delay long over them? I tell you, he will give justice to them speedily."* Sometimes, when the blessing seems to take a while, God is even then at work to bring it about in the best time and the best manner. *"If it seems slow, wait for it; it will surely come; it will not delay"* (Hab. 2:3).

God Hears Us | 23

Daily Reflections

These daily reflections are not designed to detract or add anything to Edwards' original words, but rather to allow room to ponder on what you have just read. It is a time for introspection and further Bible study to take place. Don't treat the questions rigidly to be answered methodically. They are more of a suggestion of how to digest the information. Linger on a certain question, or skip another if you so feel.

God hears us! This statement should cause us to stop and think. The fact that God hears us is often taken for granted. We very seldom stop to think that he is always there, ready to listen to our prayers. Most times, we simply pray because we have to but realizing that God is waiting to hear what we have to say to him can change the way we converse with the Almighty. It should make us more aware of what we have to say and what we expect from our prayers.

1. Do you feel that God hears you or not?
2. Why is access to God such an important aspect of prayer?
3. What is the significance of Jesus granting us access through the crucifixion? See Matt. 27:51.
4. Do you agree with the concept of God being ready to hear and answer?

7

GOD ANSWERS US

"O you who hear prayer"
Psalm 65:2

God Answers Abundantly

God hears our prayers because he answers them so freely. *"If any of you lacks wisdom, let him ask God, who gives generously to all without reproach, and it will be given him"* (Jam. 1:5-6). People often show their unwillingness to give by the inadequacy of their gifts and by finding fault with those who ask of them. But, God gives liberally and does not point out how much we do not deserve the gifts. He is generous and rich to those who call on him. *"For you, O LORD, are good and forgiving, abounding in steadfast love to all who call upon you"* (Psalm 86:5). *"For there is no distinction between Jew and Greek; for the same Lord is Lord of all, bestowing his riches on all who call on him"* (Rom. 10:12).

Sometimes, God not only gives what we ask for, but he gives us more than we ask, just as he did to Solomon. *"Behold, I now do according to your word. Behold, I give you a wise and discerning mind, so that none like you has been before you and none like you shall arise after you. I give you also what you have not asked, both riches and honor, so that no other king shall compare with you, all your days"* (1 Kings 3:12-13). God will give more to his people than they can either ask or think, as is implied in Ephesians 3:20: *"Now to him who is able to do far more abundantly than all that we ask or think."*

We can see God hears prayer because of the miracles he has often done in answer to prayer.

- Esau was coming with 400 men against his brother Jacob. To cut him off, Jacob prayed and God turned Esau's heart so that he was friendly when he met Jacob (Gen. 32).
- In Egypt, because of Moses' prayers, God brought those dreadful plagues, and because of his prayer, took them away again.
- When Samson was about to die of thirst, he prayed, and God brought water out of a hollow place (Jdg. 15:18-19). And when he prayed, after his strength had left him, God strengthened him, so he could pull down the temple of Dagon on the Philistines—those he killed at his death were more than all those he killed before.
- Joshua prayed to God, and said, *"Sun, stand still at Gibeon, and moon, in the Valley of Aijalon"* (Josh. 10:12).

And God heard his prayer and made the sun and moon stand still.

- The prophet *"Elijah was a man with a nature like ours, and he prayed fervently that it might not rain, and for three years and six months it did not rain on the earth. Then he prayed again, and heaven gave rain, and the earth bore its fruit"* (Jam. 5:17-18).
- God confused the army of Zerah, the Ethiopian, in answer to the prayer of Asa (2 Chron. 14:9).
- God sent an angel and killed 185,000 men of Sennacherib's army in answer to Hezekiah's prayer (2 Kings 19:14-16, 19, 35).

God Is Moved by Prayer

When God is displeased by sin, he shows his displeasure and seems to oppose and resist us. In such cases, God is moved by humble and passionate prayer. *"The prayer of a righteous person has great power as it is working"* (Jam. 5:16). It has great power—such a mighty God graciously shows himself as conquered by it. God appeared to oppose Jacob in what he asked for, but Jacob was persistent and overcame. Therefore, God changed his name from Jacob to Israel, because he says, *"for you have striven with God and with men, and have prevailed"* (Gen. 32:28). *"He strove with the angel and prevailed; he wept and sought his favor"* (Hos. 12:4). When God's anger was provoked against Israel, and he appeared to be ready to consume them, Moses stood in the gap, and by his humbled and sincere prayer and supplication, stopped the divine vengeance, (Exo. 32:9, Num. 14:11).

Daily Reflections

God answering prayers is sometimes a harder fact to acknowledge than him hearing us. More often than we like, our prayers seem to go unanswered, even unnoticed, and this causes many Christians to doubt, feel discouraged, and fall away from steady, persistent, faith-filled prayers. But he does answer, and when we come to accept that as gospel truth, we can come more boldly to the throne despite how long it may take to receive a reply.

1. Do you believe that God *always* answers prayer?
2. Do you believe he answers freely and abundantly?
3. Does God continue to answer in miracles as he did in the Bible? Can you think of an example?
4. What does it mean that God is 'moved' by our prayers? See 2 Chron. 33:13.
5. What kind of prayer would 'move' God?

8

WHY WE MUST PERSEVERE IN PRAYER

"To that end, keep alert with all perseverance,
making supplication for all the saints"
Ephesians 6:18

It is clear in the Bible that perseverance in our Christian walk is necessary for salvation:

- *"You meet him who joyfully works righteousness, those who remember you in your ways. Behold, you were angry, and we sinned; in our sins we have been a long time, and shall we be saved?"* (Isaiah 64:5).
- *"'My righteous one shall live by faith, and if he shrinks back, my soul has no pleasure in him.' But we are not of those who shrink back and are destroyed, but of those who have faith and preserve their souls"* (Heb. 10:38-39).

- *"Note then the kindness and the severity of God: severity toward those who have fallen, but God's kindness to you, provided you continue in his kindness. Otherwise you too will be cut off"* (Rom. 11:22).

Many people, when they think they are born again, seem to imagine that their work is done and that there is nothing else necessary to get to heaven. Perseverance in holiness is not necessary for salvation, as the righteousness by which a right to salvation is obtained. Nor is perseverance necessary for that righteousness by which we are justified. For as soon as we believed in Christ, or put faith in him, we have his righteousness, and all the promises purchased by it.

But persevering in prayer, worship, and Christian duties is necessary to salvation, as evidence of a title to salvation. There is never a title to salvation without it, though it is not the righteousness by which a title to salvation is obtained. It is necessary for salvation, as it is the necessary consequence of true faith. It is the evidence that accompanies righteousness, and not having it shows a lack of righteousness. Those who are good and upright in heart are distinguished from those who fall away or turn aside: *"Do good, O LORD, to those who are good, and to those who are upright in their hearts! But those who turn aside to their crooked ways the LORD will lead away with evildoers! Peace be upon Israel!"* (Psalm 125:4-5). It is mentioned as evidence that the hearts of the Israelites were not right with God, and that they did not persevere in the ways of holiness. *"A generation whose heart was not steadfast, whose spirit was not faithful to God"* (Psalm 78:8).

Jesus gives this as a distinguishing characteristic of those who are his disciples, who have a true and saving faith, and that is accompanied by perseverance in the obedience of his word. *"So Jesus said to the Jews who had believed him, "If you abide in my word, you are truly my disciples"* (John 8:31). It is mentioned as necessary evidence for those in Jesus: *"For we have come to share in Christ, if indeed we hold our original confidence firm to the end"* (Heb. 3:14).

Perseverance is not only necessary evidence of our salvation but also a necessary prerequisite to eternal life. It is the only way to heaven, the narrow way that leads to life. So, Jesus encourages the church of Philadelphia to persevere in holiness, because it was necessary in order for obtaining the crown. *"Hold fast what you have, so that no one may seize your crown"* (Rev. 3:11). It is necessary, not only that we should once have been walking in the way of duty, but that we are found that way when Jesus comes again. *"Blessed is that servant whom his master will find so doing when he comes"* (Luke 12:43). Holding out to the end is often the condition of actual salvation. *"But the one who endures to the end will be saved"* (Mat. 10:22). And *"Be faithful unto death, and I will give you the crown of life"* (Rev. 2:10).

Daily Reflections

These daily reflections are designed to reflect deeper into your own understanding and also to be able to see your own prayer life, and any shortcomings there might be. There is always room to grow, and by being honest with yourself in these questions, instead of exposing weaknesses, you can see areas that God wants to help you in to bring you to maturity. Take every opportunity to be real and truthful.

1. How persistent are you in prayer? If you had to rate your perseverance out of 10, where would you rank?
2. Why are perseverance in prayer and other Christian duties necessary?
3. As evidence, can you name a few people you know who exhibit this quality in their Christian lives?
4. Why do you think the Bible, and Jesus, talk and warn so much about perseverance?

9

NEGLECTING PERSONAL PRAYER

"Yet you did not call upon me, O Jacob;
but you have been weary of me, O Israel!"
Isaiah 43:22

If you neglect personal prayer, you show that you are willing to neglect all worship of God. The person who only prays when they pray with others would not pray at all if no one was watching. Those who will not pray where only God sees them clearly do not pray out of respect to God, and so disregard all prayer. What a miserable Christian who disregards the worship of God, and in effect, disregards God himself—they refuse to be conversant with him as their God.

How can you expect to live with God forever if you neglect and forsake him here on earth? By not praying, you are not placing your happiness, nearness, and communion in God. The person who refuses to visit and talk with a friend and ignores him when he is invited to come shows that he does not place his happiness in the company and conversation of that friend. Now, how can you expect to have happiness for eternity and be with God, and enjoy holy communion with him, if you ignore him?

Those people who have neglected personal prayer should think about what will profit them, to please themselves while they live with things that will not last but leave them disappointed.

The streams which have no springs to feed them will dry up. The drought and heat consume the snow waters. Although they run fully in the spring, when the sun rises higher with a burning heat, they are gone. The seed that is sown in stony places, though it seems to flourish at present, yet as the sun rises, it will wither away. Only those hearts that are good ground will bring forth fruit with patience. Without any heavenly seed remaining in them, people might continue to talk like Christians. They may tell of what they have experienced, but their actions do not match up. They may continue to tell of their experiences and yet live neglecting prayer, and other duties.

Consider how this neglect is inconsistent with leading a holy life. We are instructed in the Bible that true Christians must lead a holy life: *"and for the holiness without which no one will see the Lord"* (Heb. 12:14); *"everyone who thus hopes in him purifies himself as he is pure* (1 John 3:3). In Proverbs 16:17, it is said: *"The highway of the upright turns aside from evil."* The same is

34 | JONATHAN EDWARDS ON PRAYER

written in Isaiah 35:8: *"And a highway shall be there, and it shall be called the Way of Holiness; the unclean shall not pass over it. It shall belong to those who walk on the way."* It is spoken of in Romans 8:1, as the character of all believers, that they should not walk after the flesh, but after the Spirit.

But how is a life that is prayerless consistent with a holy life? To lead a holy life is to lead a life devoted to God; a life of worshiping and serving God; a life consecrated to the service of God. But how can we lead such a life if we do not maintain the duty of prayer? How can we be said to walk by the Spirit and to be a servant of God? A holy life is a life of faith. The life that true Christians live in the world, they live by the faith of the Son of God. But who can believe that man who lives by faith lives without prayer, which is the natural expression of faith? Prayer is as natural an expression of faith as breathing is of life, and to say a man lives a life of faith, and yet lives a prayerless life, is as inconsistent and incredible as to say that a man lives without breathing.

The person who lives like this, lives like an unbeliever, who does not call on God's name—they live a prayerless life, they live without God in the world.

Daily Reflections

Personal or private prayer is the most important kind of praying that we can be involved in, and yet we find it the hardest to maintain and the easiest to disregard when things get busy and distracting. We can carry on praying in church and in meetings, but if we do not do so on our own, when we are alone, it is meaningless. The repercussions of this are tremendous, right down to diluting our relationship with Jesus. It was Martin Luther who said, "To be a Christian without prayer is no more possible than to be alive without breathing."

1. Have you ever had a time or period in your life when personal prayer has been neglected or shelved? Why?
2. Why is this "inconsistent with leading a holy life"?
3. What kinds of things distract or pull you away from prayer the most? Is there a way to deal with this so that it doesn't hinder your quiet time?
4. Why are faith and prayerlessness incompatible?
5. How important is your personal prayer time to you?

10

IDOLS CANNOT HEAR YOUR PRAYERS

They have mouths, but do not speak; eyes, but do not see.
They have ears, but do not hear
Psalm 115:5-6

Many of those things that are worshiped as gods are idols made by their worshippers: sticks and stones that know nothing. They are made with ears, but they cannot hear the prayers of those who cry to them. They have eyes, but they cannot see.

Even if they are not man-made, they are things without life. So, many worship the sun, moon, and stars, which, though they are glorious, are not capable of knowing anything of the needs and desires of those who pray to them. Some worship animals, as the Egyptians worshiped bulls, which, though they were living, had no reason capable of knowing the requests of their worshipers. Others worship devils instead of the true God—*"what pagans sacrifice they offer to demons"* (1 Cor. 10:20). Though these beings have great power, they do not have the knowledge necessary to fully understand the state, circumstances, necessities, and desires of those who pray to them.

But the true God knows the circumstances of everyone who prays to him throughout the world. Though millions pray to him at once, in different parts of the world, it is not difficult for him, as he is infinite in knowledge and can take notice of everyone, not just one at a time. God is so perfect in knowledge that he does not need to be informed by us in order to know our needs, for he knows what we need before we ask him.

The worshipers of false gods used to lift their voices and cry aloud, in case their gods should not be able to hear them, as Elijah mocked the worshipers of Baal to do in 1 Kings 18:27. But the true God hears the silent petitions of his people. He does not need us to cry aloud—he knows and understands when we only pray in our hearts, as Hannah did in 1 Samuel 1:13.

Idols are but pretensions and lies—in them is no help. When it comes to power or knowledge, they are nothing. As Paul says, *"An idol has no real existence"* (1 Cor. 8:4). As for images and pictures, they are so far from having the power to answer prayer that they are not able to act: *"They have hands, but do not feel; feet, but do not walk; and they do not make a sound in their throat"* (Psalm 115:7). Those who make them and pray to them are senseless and foolish, and make sticks and stones in their own likeness. *"Their idols are like scarecrows in a cucumber field, and they cannot speak; they have to be carried, for they cannot walk. Do not be afraid of them, for they cannot do evil, neither is it in them to do good"* (Jer. 10:5).

As for the sun, moon, and stars, although we benefit from them, they only act by the necessity of nature. Therefore, they have no power to do anything in answer to prayers. And demons, though worshiped as gods, are not able to make those who worship them happy, and can do nothing at all but by divine permission.

When the Israelites departed and turned from God to idols, and then cried to him in their distress, he rebuked them for their foolishness by telling them to cry to their gods for deliverance from their tribulation (Jos. 10:14). So, God challenges those gods. *"Tell us what is to come hereafter, that we may know that you are gods; do good, or do harm, that we may be dismayed and terrified. Behold, you are nothing, and your work is less than nothing; an abomination is he who chooses you"* (Isa. 41:23-24).

These false gods, instead of helping those who pray to them, cannot help themselves. Demons are miserable tormented spirits. They are bound in chains of darkness for their rebellion against the true God and cannot deliver themselves. Nor do they have any more ability to help people than a pack of hungry wolves has to protect and help a flock of lambs. And those who worship and pray to them cannot receive anything good by serving them. The only reward that Satan will give them for the service which they do for him, is to devour them.

Daily Reflections

We sometimes take it for granted that God is not an idol, and yet it is always good to be reminded of the stark contrast between a hand-made artifact and a supreme, living, spiritual being. Edwards clearly draws the distinctions with biblical backing so that we are without question as to who God is. He goes further to show that natural elements, no matter how beautiful they are, and even spirits, cannot do what God can do for us. When we pray, he is alive, near, and ready to answer us.

1. What is meant by the word idol?
2. Read Colossians 3:5. Sometimes work, money, and family can become an idol—something that we place above God, but that cannot save us. Is there anything like that in your life?
3. Why do you think we, as humans, always tend to run off to idols the same way the Israelites did?
4. Idols are not just Old Testament. Read Revelation 9:20. What do you understand from this verse?

11

WHY PEOPLE STOP PRAYING

"For what is the hope of the godless when God cuts him off, when God takes away his life? Will God hear his cry when distress comes upon him?"
Job 27:8-9

Some people often continue praying for a while after they have had revelations and, through a fear of hell, call on God and persist in their personal prayer. After their hearts have softened and they feel the goodness of God or have false joy and comfort, they might continue in prayer. Having found hope, they often carry on praying on their own. For a while, they are moved by this hope and think God has delivered them from that eternal misery that they feared. Now, while this feeling toward God continues, Christian duties seem pleasant; they even enjoy approaching God in their prayer room, and think of nothing but calling on God as long as they live.

They might continue in personal prayer for a while even after the excitement has worn off because they intend to continue seeking God. Also because of their own preconceived notions, they always believe believers should carry on praying. Therefore, though they do not love praying, and grow tired of it, they reluctantly continue.

To carry on so as they have always been taught is a sign of false hope. So, even though they hate praying, and would be glad to be done with it, without wanting to look like hypocrites, they keep up the appearance of prayer. This might keep up the appearance of Christianity for a while. They will not suddenly stop because that would be too much of a shock to their false peace. But they will do this gradually, as their consciences can bear it, and as they can find out ways to cover the matter. But, false Christians, after a while, will always stop practicing prayer.

They can stop praying, and even those who know who they are, will not be aware of it so that their reputation is still intact. If others saw how they neglected it, it would shock them. But it is not noticed, at least not by many. Therefore, they leave it out and still have the credit of being born-again Christians.

People like this can neglect personal prayer in small ways without affecting their peace. Even though Christians living without private prayer is far from the idea they once had of a true believer, they find ways to change their view and bring their principles to suit their inclinations. Sooner or later, they believe that a person can be a Christian, and yet live without prayer. In time, they make many things suit themselves: a hope of heaven, an indulgence in gratifying their own appetites, and living a prayerless life. They cannot suddenly make these things agree—it happens over time. By degrees, they find ways to guard and defend their consciences against everything else so that they can co-exist well together.

1. It is not their intention, but they will often carry on with an external attendance of public prayer, or prayer with others. Many wicked people, who make no claim to serious faith, often attend public prayers in the congregation, and also more private prayers in the families in which they live, unless worldly pleasures and diversions interfere, then they make no effort to attend family prayer.

They can continue to attend these prayers as long as they live, and yet might never truly call on God, because it is not really their own prayer. They are only there for their credit, or to comply with others. They might be there but have no proper prayer of their own. Many people are like this, as it speaks of in Job 15:4: *"But you are doing away with the fear of God and hindering meditation before God."*

1. But most of them give up the practice of personal prayer. They get to this point in stages. At first, they begin to be careless about it, after being tempted

away, because they have been out with friends and other people or are distracted by worldly things. After that, they easily skip it again. So, it becomes a frequent thing for them to not do it and after a while, they seldom pray. Perhaps they do so on Sundays, and sometimes on other days. But they no longer try every day to be alone and worship God and seek His face. They sometimes pray a little to quiet their conscience, and to keep their old hope alive, because it would be shocking, even after all their subtle persuasions, to call themselves Christians, and yet to live completely without prayer. But personal and private prayer, they have mostly ignored.

Daily Reflections

Using a notebook to write down thoughts, verses, and even prayers is a very good idea. It will help you to keep track of your answers so that you can revisit them or refer to them at a later stage and see if there has been any growth in your understanding or practice of prayer. It is also useful in keeping a record of things you pray for. Sometimes we forget, but it is incredibly encouraging to reflect on those requests that have been answered. Many great men of God have followed this practice, and it helped them in their times of prayer and reflection with the Lord.

1. Why do you think some people stop praying?
2. Edwards believed that people do not just suddenly stop praying, but do so over time. Why is this so?

44 | JONATHAN EDWARDS ON PRAYER

3. Again, we find a distinction between public and personal prayer. Why is this so important?
4. What kind of things tempt us away from praying on our own?
5. Do you know people who have given up praying? What are their lives like because of it?

12

GRACE TO PRAY

"Who saved us and called us to a holy calling,
not because of our works but because of his own purpose and grace"
2 Timothy 1:9

Some people have an issue with the religious devotion of Christians who spend so much time reading, praying, singing, and hearing sermons. It is clear in the Bible that true grace causes people to delight a lot in such religious exercises.

- True grace had this effect on Anna the prophetess: *"She did not depart from the temple, worshiping with fasting and prayer night and day"* (Luke 2:37). And grace had this effect on the early Christians in Jerusalem: *"And day by day, attending the temple together and breaking bread* in their homes, they received their food with glad and generous hearts, praising God" (Acts 2:46-47). Grace made Daniel delight in praying three times a day, just as David did: "Evening and morning and at noon I utter my complaint and moan, and he hears my voice" (Psalm 55:17).

- Grace makes believers delight in singing praises to God: "Sing to his name, for it is pleasant!" (Psalm 135:3). "Praise the LORD! For it is good to sing praises to our God; for it is pleasant, and a song of praise is fitting" (Psalm 147:1).

- It also delights them to hear the word of God preached: It makes the gospel a joyful sound to them (Psalm 89:15). It makes the feet of those who bring good news, to be beautiful: "How beautiful upon the mountains are the feet of him who brings good news" (Isa. 52:7).

- It makes them love public worship: "O LORD, I love the habitation of your house and the place where your glory dwells" (Psalm 26:8). "One thing have I asked of the LORD, that will I seek after: that I may dwell in the house of the LORD all the days of my life, to gaze upon the beauty of the Lord and to inquire in his temple" (Psalm 27:4). "How lovely is your dwelling place, O LORD of hosts! My soul longs, yes, faints for the courts of the Lord; my heart and flesh sing for joy to the living God. Even the sparrow finds a home, and the swallow a nest for herself, where she may lay her young, at your altars, O LORD of hosts, my King and my God. Blessed are those who dwell in your house, ever singing your praise! Selah Blessed are those whose strength is in you, in whose heart are the highways to Zion. As they go through *the Valley of Baca they make it a place of springs; the early rain also covers it with pools. They go from strength to strength; each one appears before God in Zion... For a day in your courts is better than a thousand elsewhere"* (Psalm 84:1-10).

This is the nature of true grace.

But for people who are used to zealously engaging in the external exercises of Christianity, and who spend a lot of time in them, there is no real evidence of grace, because this behavior is found in many who have no grace. It was the same with the Israelites whose practices were abominable to God; they attended the new moons, the sabbaths, and the calling of assemblies; they stretched out their hands, and made many prayers (Isa.1:12-15). It was the same with the Pharisees who made long prayers and fasted twice a week. False religion can cause people to be loud and sincere in prayer: *"Fasting like yours this day will not make your voice to be heard on high."* (Isa. 58:4). Christianity which is not spiritual and saving can cause people to delight in religious duties and rituals: *"Yet they seek me daily and delight to know my ways, as if they were a nation that did righteousness and did not forsake the judgment of their God; they ask of me righteous judgments; they delight to draw near to God"* (Isa. 58:2).

Daily Reflections

There is a distinct difference between those who pray in grace and those who do not. Grace is defined as the free and unmerited favor of God, shown in the salvation of sinners and the gift of blessings. Or it can be remembered in the acronym: **God's Riches At Christ's Expense.** It is not something we can ever earn, but is given to us by God, undeservedly free. A true understanding of this wonderful virtue from above opens our eyes to see the privilege and wonder of prayer and praise. It triggers a spontaneous response to want to speak and sing to the Lord who continues in his giving.

1. What do you understand by the term 'grace'?
2. Why do you think it has such an effect on people, as mentioned in the verses from the Bible?
3. What kind of prayer comes from people who do not have or enjoy the grace of God?
4. Why do you think the Pharisees struggled with grace, even though they were so committed and diligent?
5. How does 2 Corinthians 9:8 apply to what we have read in this passage?

13

SEEKING GOD IN PRAYER

"And without faith it is impossible to please him,
for whoever would draw near to God must believe
that he exists and that he rewards those who seek him"
Hebrews 11:6

The good that is asked for by prayer is God himself. *"Let us go at once to entreat the favor of the Lord and to seek the Lord of hosts"* (Zech. 8:21). This is the good they ask for and seek by prayer, The Lord of hosts himself. To seek God can mean seeking the favor or mercy of God. So, praying before the Lord, and seeking the Lord of hosts, must mean the same thing.

But seeking the Lord often means something more; it implies that God himself is the good that is desired and sought after;

God's manifestations and communications of himself by his Holy Spirit. So, the psalmist desired God, thirsted after him, and sought him. *"O God, you are my God; earnestly I seek you; my soul thirsts for you; my flesh faints for you, as in a dry and weary land where there is no water. So I have looked upon you in the sanctuary, beholding your power and glory... My soul clings to you"* (Psalm 63:1, 2, 8). And therefore, we see the character of believers in those who seek God. *"Such is the generation of those who seek him"* (Psalm 24:6). *"You who seek God, let your hearts revive"* (Psalm 69:32).

If the meaning in the verse is understood like this, then by seeking the Lord of hosts, we must understand that God, who had withdrawn or hid himself for a long time, would return and bless them with his presence and his Spirit, which he had often promised, and for which his church had waited for a long time.

So, God's people seeking, by sincere prayer, the promised restoration of the church is called their seeking God, and searching for him; and God's granting this promised revival is called his being found by them. *"For thus says the Lord: When seventy years are completed for Babylon, I will visit you, and I will fulfill to you my promise and bring you back to this place. For I know the plans I have for you, declares the Lord, plans for welfare and not for evil, to give you a future and a hope. Then you will call upon me and come and pray to me, and I will hear you. You will seek me and find me, when you seek me with all your heart. I will be found by you, declares the Lord, and I will restore your fortunes and gather you from all the nations and all the places where I have driven you, declares the Lord, and I will bring you back to the place from which I sent you into exile"* (Jer. 29:10-14).

And when God, in answer to their prayers, delivers, restores, and advances his church, according to his promise, then he is said to answer, and come, and say, Here I am, and will show himself. Then they are said to find him and see him clearly. *"Then you shall call, and the LORD will answer; you shall cry, and he will say, 'Here I am'"* (Isa. 58:9). *"I did not say to the offspring of Jacob, 'Seek me in vain'"* (Isa. 45:19).

"'Therefore my people shall know my name. Therefore in that day they shall know that it is I who speak; here I am.' How beautiful upon the mountains are the feet of him who brings good news, who publishes peace, who brings good news of happiness, who publishes salvation, who says to Zion, 'Your God reigns.' The voice of your watchmen— they lift up their voice; together they sing for joy; for eye to eye they see the return of the LORD to Zion" (Isa. 52:6-8).

Daily Reflections

We hear and know the word 'seek,' but it seems to have lost its potency and fallen out of use in modern English, except when it comes to the children's game of hide-and-seek! The meaning is still the same here, since it calls for us to look, and keep on looking, until we find what we are after. It is like this with prayer when we seek the Lord. We should continue to press in for that which we want and desire.

1. Read 1 Chronicles 22:19 and 2 Chronicles 7:14. These are clear calls by God to seek him. Why do you think it was so important for God to command us to do this?

2. What did Paul mean in Acts 17:27? What did God do to make people seek after him?
3. Read Hebrews 11:6. What rewards are there for those who seek?
4. What kind of seeking is spoken of in Jeremiah 29:13?
5. Read Proverbs 8:17. What is the promise given to those who seek God?

14

CAN CHILDREN PRAY IN MEETINGS?

"Out of the mouth of infants and nursing babies you have prepared praise"
Matthew 21:16

Not everyone agrees on children's participation in reading and praying together in meetings, or Christian duties by themselves. They object to children's lack of knowledge and discretion, which is necessary for ordered and profitable management of religious exercises. But this objection is not sufficient.

Children, who are capable of fellowship with each other, are capable of the influence of the Spirit of God in its active fruits. And if they have a Christian nature, which they have from the Spirit of God, in order to improve their fellowship in a religious manner and for religious purposes, who should stop them? If they do not have the discretion to observe correct methods in what they do or to speak sense in all that they say in prayer, they might have a good meaning, and God understands them, and it does not spoil or interrupt their devotion with each other.

As adults, we have defects in our prayers that are a thousand times worse in the sight of God and are a greater confusion, a more absurd nonsense in His eyes, than their childish indiscretions. There is not much difference before God between children and grown-ups, as we think. We are all poor, ignorant, foolish babies in his sight. Our adult age does not bring us closer to God, as we often think.

God, in this work, has shown remarkable regard for little children. He has been pleased to perfect praise out of their mouths, and many of them have more of that knowledge and wisdom that pleases him, and he sees their worship as more acceptable than many of the great, educated men of the world. The adults, in the sight of God, are the ignorant and foolish children. I hope for the days prophesied in Isaiah 65:20, when *"the young man shall die a hundred years old."*

I have seen many wonderful results of children's religious meetings, and God has seemed to move in and through them in their meetings, and really descended from heaven to be amongst them. I have known several examples of children being born again at such meetings. I should therefore think that if children appear to be really moved to it by Christian nature, and not merely from a childish emotion of imitating grown-ups, they should not be discouraged or put off.

But, it is good that care should be taken of these children by their parents and pastors to instruct and direct them, and to correct improper conduct and irregularities if they are noticed, or anything that the devil may pervert and destroy in their meetings.

Everyone should see that they do not find fault with or despise the Christianity of children from an evil principle; otherwise, they would be like the chief priests and scribes who were very upset with the religious worship and praises of little children, and the honor they gave Jesus in the temple in Matthew 21:15-16. In this story, we also have Jesus' response when he noticed their displeasure:

But when the chief priests and the scribes saw the wonderful things that he did, and the children crying out in the temple, "Hosanna to the Son of David!" they were indignant, and they said to him, "Do you hear what these are saying?" And Jesus said to them, "Yes; have you never read, 'Out of the mouth of infants and nursing babies you have prepared praise'?"

Daily Reflections

Children are often forgotten or overlooked when it comes to church and Christianity. We know that they are people with souls and hearts, but for some reason, because they are immature in age, we assume that they are also not ready in the spirit. But there are many adults who are far more childish in their spiritual states than those children who are serious about their walk with the Lord. Just as Jesus told the disciples, so we should not stop these little ones from coming to the Lord, even in our church meetings!

1. What is the view of children in your church meetings? Is there a place for them?
2. Do you think God honors children's prayers less or more highly than adults?
3. Why do you think we are told to be more like children in our belief and faith—Matthew 18:3-4?
4. What is the significance of Matthew 18:5?
5. Read Luke 22:26. How can the greatest become like the youngest in prayer?

15

REASONS HYPOCRITES DO NOT PRAY

"Will he take delight in the Almighty?
Will he call upon God at all times?"
Job 27:10

1. Hypocrites never had the spirit of prayer given to them. They may have been stirred up in doing it externally, yet never had the true spirit. The spirit of prayer is a holy, gracious spirit that we read about in Zech. 12:10: *"And I will pour out on the house of David and the inhabitants of Jerusalem a spirit of grace and pleas for mercy."* Wherever there is a true spirit of supplication, there is the spirit of grace.

The true spirit of prayer is God's own Spirit dwelling in the hearts of believers. And as it comes from God, it returns to God in holy sighs and groans. It naturally leads to God, to converse with Him in prayer. Therefore, the Spirit is said to make intercession for us with groanings that cannot be uttered (Rom. 8:26).

1. Someone who is truly born again sees themself as a poor, empty, helpless creature, and they stand in continual need of God's help. They know that without God, they can do nothing. A false conversion makes a person self-sufficient in their own eyes. They say they are rich and need nothing, but do not know that they are miserable, poor, blind, and naked. After a true conversion, the soul remains aware of its own impotence and emptiness, and its dependence on God for everything. There are new desires which were never there before; holy appetites, a hungering and thirsting after righteousness, a longing after more acquaintance and communion with God.

2. The command to pray is very clear:

   - *"Watch and pray that you may not enter into temptation"* (Matt. 26:41).
   - *"Praying at all times in the Spirit, with all prayer and supplication. To that end, keep alert with all perseverance, making supplication for all the saints"* (Eph. 6:18).
   - *"But when you pray, go into your room and shut the door and pray to your Father who is in secret"* (Matt. 6:6).

As long as the hypocrite was aware of the danger of hell, they dared not disobey these commands. But since they think they are now safe from hell, they neglect the clearest command in the Bible.

1. Often, hypocrites will return to sinful habits, which keeps them from praying. While they were convicted, they changed their lives. This reformation continues for a while after their supposed conversion, while they are filled with hope and false comfort. But as these things die away, their old lusts revive, and they soon return like the dog to its vomit and the pig that was clean to its wallowing in the mud. They return to their sensual, worldly habits, to their proud and contentious ways. And no wonder this makes them leave the prayer room. Sinning and praying do not agree. If a person is constantly in personal prayer, it will restrain them from deliberate sinning. So, on the other hand, if they allow themselves to sin, it will stop them from praying.

A person who knows that they live in sin against God will not be inclined to come daily into the presence of God; but will rather flee from His presence, as Adam ran away and hid when he had eaten the forbidden fruit. To keep praying after indulging their lusts would upset a person's conscience. It would give their conscience a chance to testify against them. Therefore, hypocrites, when they admit their wicked habits, exclude prayer.

1. Hypocrites never counted the cost of perseverance in seeking God and of following Him all their lives. To continue in prayer like this requires care, watchfulness, and effort. There is much opposition against praying by the world and the devil, and Christians are often tempted to give it up. To persevere in prayer, you must persevere in all Christianity. But hypocrites never count the cost of such effort. It is no surprise when they are tired that, after they have continued for a while, they find that prayer becomes annoying and tedious.

2. Hypocrites have no interest in those promises which God made to His people about those spiritual things which are necessary to keep them in prayer to the end. God has promised true Christians that he will *"put the fear of me in their hearts, that they may not turn from me"* (Jer. 32:40). He has promised to keep them in Christian duties: *"Now may the God of peace himself sanctify you completely, and may your whole spirit and soul and body be kept blameless at the coming of our Lord Jesus Christ. He who calls you is faithful; he will surely do it"* (1 Thess. 5:23-24).

But hypocrites have no interest in these promises and, therefore, are liable to fall away. If God does not uphold them, there is no guarantee for their steadfastness. If the Spirit of God departs from them, they will soon become careless, and their devotion will come to an end.

Daily Reflections

Have your Bible close when you spend time reading these chapters. You will notice that Edwards enjoyed backing up his words with many scriptures. Although most of them are written out for you to read, others are simply referenced. It is good to go and check them and treat this as a sort of Bible study. It is one of the ways we grow in our biblical knowledge. You may even be reminded of another verse that pertains to the passage we are reading—look it up. This is one of the ways God speaks to us—through his Word.

1. What is your definition of a hypocrite?
2. Read Luke 6:46 and Galatians 6:3 in the context of hypocrisy. What do you understand by these verses?
3. What is the reward for hypocrisy? Read Matthew 6:1.
4. Why is prayer such a difficult thing for hypocrites to continue in?
5. What other aspects of Christianity are neglected, other than prayer?

16

A CRY GOD WILL NOT HEAR

For he says,
"In a favorable time I listened to you, and in a day of salvation I have
helped you." Behold, now is the favorable time; behold, now is the day
of salvation
2 Corinthians 6:2

God has put himself under no obligation, by any promise, to keep any person out of hell. He has made no promises of eternal life or any deliverance from eternal death but to those in the covenant of grace, the promises given in Jesus. But anyone who is not a child of the covenant has no interest in these promises; they do not believe in them, and have no interest in the Mediator of the covenant.

So, whatever promises people think were made seeking and knocking, whatever efforts and prayers are made, until a person believes in Jesus, God is under no obligation to keep them from eternal destruction.

So, people who are not in Jesus are held in the hand of God over hell; they deserve the fiery pit and are already sentenced to it. God is provoked, his anger toward them is as though they are actually already suffering his judgment in hell, and they have done nothing to appease or abate that anger. God is not, in any way, bound by any promise to hold them up for one moment. The devil is waiting for them, hell is gaping for them, the flames gather and flash about them and would lay hold of them and swallow them up. The fire in their own hearts is struggling to break out, and they have no interest in any Mediator. There are no means within their reach that can be any security to them. In short, they have no refuge, nothing to take hold of. All that preserves them every moment is the will and uncovenanted, unobligated patience of an incensed God.

The sovereign pleasure of God, for now, holds back his rough wind; otherwise, it would come with fury, and destruction would come like a whirlwind, and those people would be like the chaff of wheat on the threshing floor.

And there is no other reason why they have not dropped into hell since they woke up in the morning, except that God's hand has held them up. There is no other reason to be given why they have not gone to hell, since they have sat in church, provoking him by their sinful, wicked manner of attending his holy worship.

64 | JONATHAN EDWARDS ON PRAYER

Now, God stands ready to pity you. This is a day of mercy; you may cry now with some encouragement that you will receive mercy. But, when the day of mercy is past, your terrible, mournful cries and shrieks will be in vain. You will be completely lost and thrown away from God, with no more regard for your welfare. God will have nothing else for you but to let you suffer in misery. There will be no other result for you, because you will be a vessel of judgment sentenced to destruction, and there will be no other use for this vessel but to be filled with judgment. God will be so far from pitying you when you cry to him, his only reply is, *"I also will laugh at your calamity; I will mock when terror strikes you"* (Prov. 1:26). If you cry to God to pity you, he will be so far from pitying you in your terrible state, and show you the least regard or favor, that instead, he will only tread you under foot.

This acceptable year of the Lord, a day of such great favor to some, will also be a day of incredible judgment for others.

Daily Reflections

This chapter may come across as a very harsh reminder of hell and what is waiting for those who do not accept Jesus as their savior. It is! And yet, Edwards, when he delivered this famous sermon entitled *Sinners in the Hands of an Angry God*, did not shout and bring down fire and brimstone on his congregation. Instead, he was clear, logical, and spoke with an ordered voice. It is not how it is delivered that hits us hard, but the brevity of the message! It should wake us up to see our own state, and to see the state of others around us so that we may pray for our own soul and the souls of the lost.

1. The statement Edwards makes about God not being obliged to keep us from hell is not an easy one to accept. Do you agree with it?
2. Do you ever think of hell? Does your church ever mention it as a reality?
3. Although this is a harsh reminder of eternal damnation without Christ, there is also encouragement. What is it?
4. Does your heart move with compassion for those who still do not know Jesus?
5. Can you recall your own salvation? When was it, and how did it happen?

17

THE PRAYER OF PSALM 139

"Search me, O God, and know my heart!
Try me and know my thoughts!
And see if there be any grievous way in me,
and lead me in the way everlasting!"
Psalm 139:23-24

This psalm is a meditation on the omniscience of God—a perfect view and knowledge of everything, from the psalmist's sitting and rising up and his thoughts from far off; and of his words, *"Even before a word is on my tongue, behold, O LORD, you know it altogether"* (Psalm 139:4). Then he shows the impossibility of fleeing from God's presence, or of hiding from him; so that if he should go to heaven, hide in hell, or fly to the ends of the sea, he would still not be hidden from God. Or if he should try to hide himself in darkness, it would not cover him, because the darkness and light are the same to God.

Then he shows God's omniscience by the knowledge God had of him while he was in his mother's womb. *"My frame was not hidden from you, when I was being made in secret, intricately woven in the depths of the earth. Your eyes saw my unformed substance; in your book were written, every one of them"* (Psalm 139:15-16).

After this, the psalmist observes the consequence of this omniscience of God—he will kill the wicked since he sees all their evil, and nothing is hidden from him. The psalmist continues this meditation on God's all-seeing eye by begging God to search and try him, to see if there is any wicked way in him, and lead him in the way everlasting.

Three things can be seen in the words:

1. The act of mercy which the psalmist begs God to do for him—that God would search him. *"Search me, O God, and know my heart! Try me and know my thoughts!"*
2. How he wants to be searched—*"See if there be any grievous way in me."* This does not mean that the psalmist wants God to search him for God's own understanding. What he had said before, of God's knowing all things, implies that God has no need of that. The psalmist had said, in the second verse, that God understood his thoughts from far off—it was all plain before him, he saw it without difficulty, or without being forced to come near, and to diligently

observe. That which is plain to be seen can be seen at a distance.

Therefore, when the psalmist prays that God would search him to see if there is any evil way in him, he cannot mean that he should search that he might see or be informed, but that the psalmist might see and be informed. He prays that God would search him with his discovering light; that he would bring him to discern himself and see whether there is any wicked way in him.

Such figurative expressions are often used in the Bible. The word of God is said to be a discerner of the thoughts and intents of the heart. Not that the word itself discerns, but it searches and opens our hearts to see so that it enables us to discern the attitude and desires of our hearts. So, God is often said to try men. He does not try them for his own information, but the discovery and manifestation of them to themselves or others.

1. Observe how he wants God to search him—*"and lead me in the way everlasting!"* That means not only in a way which may have seemed right for a while, and in which he may have peace and quietness for that time, but in the way which will hold firm, stand the test, which he may confidently abide by forever, always approve of as good and right, and in which he may always have peace and joy. It is said that *"the way of the wicked will perish"* (Psalm 1:6). But the psalmist's prayer is to be led in the way of the righteous that will last forever.

Daily Reflections

There are many prayers in the book of Psalms. This is no surprise considering they are all songs of worship or prayers written to God. For most Christians, we gravitate toward the psalms because they are a real and true expression—heartfelt, raw, desperate, and exultant. We all seem to have our favorites that we use in worship and prayer. Psalm 139 is a special example of this. Not only is it filled with stunning imagery and language that stretches to the extremes, but it also has moments of deep tenderness.

1. What psalms are your favorites in times of trouble or in times of joy?
2. Why do you think God's omniscience is such an important aspect of Psalm 139 in relation to the last few lines (verses 23-24)?
3. What is meant by the words, *"Search me and know me"*?
4. What 'grievous' ways is the psalmist wanting God to identify and find? Why?
5. What is the "way everlasting"?

18

PRAYER IS HOLY

"I desire then that in every place the men should pray, lifting holy hands"
1 Timothy 2:8

Spiritual practices are holy for the following reasons:

1. They are completely and immediately about God, and things spiritual. When we take part in the acts of spiritual worship, we are in the special presence of God. When we pray and worship God, we are said to come before God, and to come into his presence: *"Come and stand before me in this house, which is called by my name"* (Jer. 7:10). *"Come into his presence with singing!"* (Psalm 100:2).

In spiritual duties, we have immediate communication with God, either in appealing to him, as in prayer and singing praises, or in receiving from him, waiting solemnly and immediately on him for spiritual good, as in hearing the word; or in both appealing to God and receiving from him, as in the communion. These were all appointed on purpose that in them we might converse and communicate with God. We are poor, ignorant, blind worms of the dust, and God saw that correspondence with God should not be left to ourselves, but he has given us these ways and means of conversing with him.

In these exercises, holy and spiritual things are exhibited and represented. In the preaching of the word, holy Doctrine and the divine will are shown; in the table of the Lord, Jesus and his benefits are represented; in prayer and praise are represented our faith, love, and obedience.

1. The goal of God's practices is holy. The immediate goal is to glorify God. They are given to direct us in the holy exercises of faith and love, godly fear and reverence, submission, thankfulness, holy joy and sorrow, holy desires, resolutions, and hopes. True worship consists of these holy and spiritual exercises; and as these spiritual practices are ones of worship, they are to help us and direct us in this kind of worship.

2. They have been given and ordered by God's authority. They not only deal with a spiritual and holy object, and are designed to direct and help us in

spiritual and holy exercises, but they have a spiritual and holy author. The infinitely great and holy God has appointed them, the eternal Three in One. Each person in the Trinity has been a part of it.

God the Father has appointed them by his own Son. They are of Jesus' own appointment; he appointed, as he had received of the Father: *"For I have not spoken on my own authority, but the Father who sent me has himself given me a commandment—what to say and what to speak"* (John 12:49). And the Father and Son endorsed them by the Spirit; they are revealed by the inspiration of the Holy Spirit.

They are holy, in that God has consecrated them. They deal with holy things; and God ordained them, that in them we might be handling holy things. They are for holy use; and it is God who, by his own immediate authority, ordained them for that holy use; which makes them more sacred.

1. They are done and performed in the name of God. So, we are commanded to do all that we do, in word or deed, in the name of Jesus. In Colossians 3:17, we understand this with respect to spiritual practices like prayer and praise. They are done in the name of God. When the word is preached by authorized ministers, they speak in God's name, as Jesus' ambassadors, and as co-workers together with Christ. *"Therefore, we are ambassadors for Christ"* (2 Cor. 5:20). *"Working together with him"* (2 Cor. 6:1). When a true minister preaches, he speaks the words of God

(1 Pet. 4:11) and he is to be heard as one representing Christ.

So, the minister represents the person of Jesus; he baptizes in his name, and in the Lord's supper stands in his place. On the other hand, the congregation, in their addresses to God in prayer and praise, act in the name of Jesus, the Mediator, as having him to represent them, and as coming to God by him.

Daily Reflections

Unfortunately, prayer is often dumbed down to our level, where we see it as desperate cries for help or some kind of elevated conversation on another level. Sometimes nothing more than a high-profile business transaction! But the reality is that it is holy and divine. It is not just something to do because we are Christians. It is communion with the Almighty, a place where we come into the holy of holies before the Holy God with our supplications and thanksgivings. When we see it like that, it should change our perception and the manner in which we approach the Lord in our times of prayer.

1. What is your definition of holy? How does this relate to prayer?
2. Read Hebrews 10:19. The throne room of God is accessible to us as it was not in the Old Covenant. How does this change things for us in prayer?
3. Why is it so significant that God, in three persons, is involved in prayer being made holy?

4. If prayer is holy, then what is our role in bringing our prayer to God? Read 1 Peter 1:16.
5. Why is praying in the name of Jesus so important? How does it change prayer?

19

PRAYING AGAINST TEMPTATION

"And lead us not into temptation, but deliver us from evil"
Matthew 6:13

We want God, in his providence toward us, not to allow those things that hurt or expose us. Therefore, we should avoid those things that lead to sin against him.

We desire and love to have God's providence toward us, so that our welfare may be secured. No one loves to live exposed, uncertain, and in dangerous circumstances. While we are like that, we live uncomfortably, in constant fear. We want God to order things concerning us that we may be safe from fear of evil, and that no evil may come near our house, and because we are afraid of disaster. So, we do not like to see or feel it near us, and love to have it far from us. We want God to be a wall of fire round about us, to defend us; that he would surround us as the mountains do the valleys, to guard us against every danger, or enemy; that no evil may come near us.

Now, this clearly shows that in our behavior toward God, we should keep far away from sin, and from everything to do with it, just as we want God to keep disaster and misery far from us and not to bring those things that expose our needs.

As we are to pray that we may not be led into temptation, we should obviously not run into it by ourselves—this is one request that Jesus directs us to make to God in the prayer that he taught his disciples—"*Lead us not into temptation.*" And how inconsistent it would be of us if we prayed to God that we should not be led into temptation, and at the same time, we were not careful to avoid temptation but brought ourselves into it by doing those things that lead and expose us to sin. What self-contradiction is it, for a man to pray to God that he may be kept from that which he takes no care to avoid! By praying that we may be kept from temptation, we admit to God that being in temptation is something to be avoided. But by running into it, we show that we choose the contrary—not to avoid it.

A better awareness of our own weakness to give in to temptation obliges us to avoid that which leads or exposes us to sin. Whoever knows himself, and is aware of how weak he is, and his constant danger of running into sin; how full of corruption his heart is, which, like fuel, is ready to catch fire and bring destruction on him; how much he has in him to draw him to sin, and how unable he is to stand by himself; who is aware of this and understands his duty—will he not be vigilant against everything that may lead and expose him to sin?

So, Jesus directed us to *"watch and pray that you may not enter into temptation"* (Matt. 26:41). The reason he gives is because the flesh is weak! The person who, in the confidence of his own strength, boldly runs the chance of sinning by going into temptation shows a foolish lack of awareness of his own weakness. *"Whoever trusts in his own mind is a fool"* (Prov. 28:26).

The wisest and strongest, and some of the holiest people in the world, have fallen because of this. So was David; so was Solomon—his wives turned his heart away. If these people who are so mighty and holy were led this way into sin, surely it should be a warning to us. *"Therefore let anyone who thinks that he stands take heed lest he fall"* (1 Cor. 10:12).

Daily Reflections

We all face temptation. There is no way around it! No matter your spiritual maturity or how many years you have been a Christian, temptation is something every person faces—even Jesus! We are not disqualified because we are tempted, only when we follow into sin. Where we need help is to not fall into the trap, not to be led into that temptation, but to be delivered from it. Jesus faced temptation and prayed that he would be given the strength not to fail in his duty.

78 | JONATHAN EDWARDS ON PRAYER

1. What does it mean when Jesus warns us to "watch and pray" against temptation?
2. Do you find it easy to pray when you face temptation or not?
3. Read 1 Corinthians 10:13. What encouragement do you get from this?
4. What is the contradiction many people face when praying against temptation?
5. What causes people to fall according to Edwards in this chapter?

20

REVIVAL PRAYER

"Thus says the LORD of hosts: Peoples shall yet come, even the inhabitants of many cities. The inhabitants of one city shall go to another, saying, 'Let us go at once to entreat the favor of the LORD and to seek the LORD of hosts; I myself am going.' Many peoples and strong nations shall come to seek the LORD of hosts in Jerusalem and to entreat the favor of the LORD"
Zechariah 8:20-22

In the passage, we have an account of how revival in the church should be introduced; by many people in different towns and countries coming in agreement that they will, united in prayer, seek God to come and show himself with his gracious presence. This prophecy talks about a great revival of Christianity, and of the true worship of God among his people, others joining the church, and turning many from idolatry to the worship of the true God.

It is evident in the Bible that there is still to be a great revival in Christianity and the kingdom of Jesus in this world by an abundant outpouring of the Spirit of God, far greater and more extensive than there has ever been. It is clear that many things, which are spoken concerning a glorious time of the church's growth and prosperity in the end days, have not yet been fulfilled.

Jesus teaches us to seek this above all other things, to make it the first and the last in our prayers, and that every petition should be for the advance of God's kingdom and glory in the world. Apart from the Lord's prayer, if we look through the whole Bible and observe all the examples of prayer, we will not find many prayers for any other blessing, as for the deliverance, restoration, and prosperity of the church, and the advancement of God's glory and kingdom of grace in the world.

1. A revival will start and be brought about through prayer. Prayer can be taken to mean general worship, since it was a main part of worship in the days of the gospel when sacrifices were abolished. But there is more to prayer than just general worship. It is clearly and repeatedly mentioned when it comes to prophecies that speak of a spirit of prayer, as preceding and introducing revival. Just look at the verses in Zechariah 12:10 about the pouring out of a spirit of grace and supplication, with which this great revival of Christianity shall begin.

2. Prayer will be immediate and ongoing. *"Let us go at once"* can also mean 'Let us go continually.' The words literally translated are, 'Let us go in going.' This doubling of words is very common in the Hebrew language when something must be strongly expressed. It generally implies the superlative degree of something—as the holy of holies signifies the most holy. It not only describes the utmost degree of something but also the utmost certainty—as when God said to Abraham, *"In multiplying, I will multiply thy seed"* (Gen. 22:17 KJV). It implies that God would certainly multiply his seed, and also multiply it exceedingly.

So when the meaning of the verse is, "Let us go in going, and pray before the Lord," the strength of the expression represents the sincerity of those who make the proposal, and how much they are engaged in it. And for those who receive the proposal, it can be understood to signify that they should be quick, passionate, and constant in it; or, that it should be performed thoroughly—done well.

1. We can learn from this prophecy, in its context, that this prayer will be a joyful occasion, acceptable to God, and attended with glorious success.

We can assume from the passage that it will be pleasing to God, for many people, in different parts of the world, will agree to come together in extraordinary, immediate, sincere, and constant prayer, led by the Holy Spirit. This will bring about the revival of Jesus' church and kingdom, which God has so often promised will be in the end days of the world. And so, I encourage Christians to come together in extraordinary prayer for this great blessing.

Daily Reflections

As Christians, we all wish for revival, a fresh outpouring of the Holy Spirit, and a renewal of our passion and fire for Jesus. But this does not happen without prayer. God seems to hold his hand until he sees our desperate want for it. In fact, in almost every great revival, it is well documented that serious prayer preceded them. A group of determined and committed people sought the Lord to come and quicken the hearts of those in the church and those who have not yet been born again.

1. What is your idea of a revival in the church? Is it local or global?
2. Do you ever think or pray for revival or is that something that is allocated to others in the church?
3. Read Psalm 80:19. What does 'saved' mean in this context for Christians?
4. What do you understand when Edwards says "spirit of prayer" in terms of a revival?
5. What is the meaning of the Hebrew translation of the verse: "Let us go in going"?

21

UNITY IN REVIVAL PRAYER

"Thus says the LORD of hosts: Peoples shall yet come, even the inhabitants of many cities. The inhabitants of one city shall go to another, saying, 'Let us go at once to entreat the favor of the LORD and to seek the LORD of hosts; I myself am going.' Many peoples and strong nations shall come to seek the LORD of hosts in Jerusalem and to entreat the favor of the LORD"
Zechariah 8:20-22

Who Will Come Pray?

Who will be united in prayer, seeking God for a revival in the last days? The inhabitants of many cities and many countries, great crowds in different parts of the world, will come to pray. From the prophecy, it appears logical that it will be fulfilled in this way: There will be a spirit of prayer on God's people, in many places, bringing them into an agreement, united to pray to God that he would come and help his church, and in mercy, pour out his Spirit, revive his work, and advance his spiritual kingdom in the world, as he has promised.

This manner of prayer, and the unity in it, will increase until there is a revival in the worship and service of God amongst Christians. This will cause others to become aware of the needs of their souls, and bring a great concern for their spiritual and eternal beings until they cry to God for spiritual blessings, and join in seeking and serving God.

In this way, Christianity will grow until the revival reaches those in prominent positions, whole nations are stirred, and many countries join the church. So, after the inhabitants of many cities of Israel have agreed to go and pray before the Lord, and seek the Lord of hosts, others shall be drawn to worship and serve him with them; until many people and strong nations join them, and the church will increase so that it shall be ten times as large as it was before. Thus *"ten men from the nations of every tongue shall take hold of the robe of a Jew, saying, 'Let us go with you, for we have heard that God is with you"* (Zech. 8:23). *"O you who hear prayer, to you shall all flesh come"* (Psalm 65:2).

How Will They Come?

It will be a visible unity, in agreement with each other. The inhabitants of one city shall ask others, saying, *"Let us go."* They will agree and more will follow, it will be something that spreads; one following another's example, saying, "I will also go."

It is logical that these words are not those people inviting others, but of those to whom the proposal is made, or the reply of those agreeing to go with it. This makes sense in the context because of the number of people following and taking hold of the robes of those who are Jews.

We can understand that there will be many from other cities that join in, even though it does not say this. We can see the same thing in Jeremiah 3:22: *"'Return, O faithless sons; I will heal your faithlessness.' 'Behold, we come to you, for you are the LORD our God.'"*

Daily Reflections

Following on from the chapter before this one, the focus is on praying for revival. But this is discussed with a focus on unity among those who are involved. Without unity, the power of their prayers is negated. When the people are in agreement, in their spirits and their hearts, then their pleas reach the throne of God and are effective in opening his hand. This unity, though, is not just a consensus, but a oneness in reaching the goal of spiritual renewal in people's lives.

1. This verse in Zechariah is very interesting as it portrays a gathering of people beyond just your local church. Who is it talking about?
2. Where does this unity among people who do not know each other come from?
3. Read 2 Corinthians 13:11 in terms of unity in revival. What does this verse mean?

4. Does the aspect of a visible unity excite you? How do you think this will happen?
5. Is there anyone in your church busy praying for a revival right now?

22

SECRET PRAYER

"But when you pray, go into your room and shut the door and pray to your Father who is in secret. And your Father who sees in secret will reward you"
Matthew 6:6

A true Christian loves Christian fellowship and Christian conversation, and their heart is engaged in it. But they also love to retire from people to converse with God in solitary places. This also has advantages for focusing their heart and engaging its emotions. True Christianity is where people will be alone in solitary places for holy meditation and prayer. So it was with Isaac in Genesis 24:63. It was the same with Jesus. How often we read of his going off into the mountains and solitary places to talk with his Father!

88 | JONATHAN EDWARDS ON PRAYER

It is difficult to hide emotions, although holy emotions are much more silent and secret than fake ones. So it is with the sorrow of Christians for their own sins. The mourning of those truly repentant is represented as being so secret—hidden from others. *"The land shall mourn, each family by itself: the family of the house of David by itself, and their wives by themselves; the family of the house of Nathan by itself, and their wives by themselves; the family of the house of Levi by itself, and their wives by themselves; the family of the Shimeites by itself, and their wives by themselves; and all the families that are left, each by itself, and their wives by themselves"* (Zech. 12:12-14).

It is like this with their sorrow for the sins of others. *"But if you will not listen, my soul will weep in secret for your pride; my eyes will weep bitterly and run down with tears, because the Lord's flock has been taken captive"* (Jer. 13:17). It is like this with joy—it is like hidden manna (Rev. 2:17). The Psalms speak of comfort as being in secret. *"My soul will be satisfied as with fat and rich food, and my mouth will praise you with joyful lips, when I remember you upon my bed, and meditate on you in the watches of the night"* (Psalm 63:5-6).

Jesus calls his bride out from the world, into solitary places, that he may give her his love. *"Come, my beloved, let us go out into the fields and lodge in the villages... There I will give you my love"* (Song 7:11-12). The most precious blessings people obtained in the Bible were when they were on their own.

- God showed his covenant blessings to Abraham when he was alone, away from his family. Isaac received the gift of Rebekah while he was walking alone, meditating in the field.

- Jacob was alone in secret prayer when Jesus came, wrestled with him, and blessed him.
- God revealed himself to Moses in the bush, when he was alone in the desert (Exod. 3). And when God showed Moses his glory, the closest communion he ever had with God, he was alone on the mountain, where he stayed forty days and forty nights before coming down with his face shining.
- God came to Elijah and Elisha and talked with them when they were alone.
- And when Jesus was transfigured, it was not in a crowd but in a solitary place with only three disciples, telling them that they should tell no one until he had risen from the dead.
- When the angel Gabriel came to Mary, and the Holy Spirit came on her, she seems to have been alone. Joseph, to whom she was engaged, knew nothing about it. And the woman who first shared the joy of Christ's resurrection was alone with him at the tomb (John 20).
- And when John was given visions of Jesus and his future dispensations toward the church and the world, he was alone on Patmos.

There were also times of great privileges when the believers received when with others. There is also a great blessing in Christian conversation and public worship that refreshes the hearts of Christians. But it is the nature of true grace that, although it loves Christian fellowship, it flourishes in secret conversations with God. So, if people appear greatly engaged in social Christianity, but have little time in the prayer room on their own—if they are motivated when with others but are hardly moved when there is no one but God and Jesus to talk to—it will not show well in their faith.

Daily Reflections

Secret prayer or time alone with God is one of the most important aspects of our relationship with him. Years ago the term 'closet' was used but now we refer to a prayer room, and the act of closing yourself off from the busy activities and other people in your house is still the same as in Jesus' day. He just found it more useful to go into nature, since he was often traveling from town to town. For us, finding a quiet spot to come aside with the Lord is just as important as speaking and hearing from God.

1. Do you have a daily habit of praying on your own in a 'secret' place?
2. Why is it so important to pray in secret or in a place where no one else can see or hear you?
3. In Matthew 6:6 it says that our Father in heaven will reward us if we pray in secret. What do you think this reward is?
4. Which of the biblical examples in the chapter do you identify with, if any? Why?
5. How does faith exhibit itself in us if we spend time on our own praying or not?

23

PRAYING FOR THE LOST AS JESUS DID

"When he went ashore he saw a great crowd, and he had compassion on them, because they were like sheep without a shepherd"
Mark 6:34

P astors should follow the example of Jesus in the way they seek the salvation and happiness of the souls of people.

They should follow his example of love for souls; though it is impossible that they can love them to such a great degree, they should have the same spirit of love and concern for their salvation. Love for people's souls in Jesus was far above any regard he had for his physical needs and his honor. It should be the same for his ministers. They should have the same spirit of compassion for the people that he had. *"When he went ashore he saw a great crowd, and he had compassion on them, because they were like sheep without a shepherd. And he began to teach them many things."*

"Had compassion" means that he was affected, moved with pity. And again we read in Luke 19 that when Jesus was riding to Jerusalem a few days before his crucifixion and came to the Mount of Olives where he had a view of the city, he wept over it, because of the misery and ruin they had brought themselves into for their sin.

The sin they were guilty of was their terrible treatment of him, and even though he knew how he would be arrested, bound, falsely accused and condemned, reviled, spat on, whipped, and crucified, it did not prevent his affectionate tears of compassion toward them. *"And when he drew near and saw the city, he wept over it, saying, "Would that you, even you, had known on this day the things that make for peace! But now they are hidden from your eyes"* (Luke 19:41-42). Compare with Matt. 23:37 and Luke 13:34.

One would have thought he would have been more concerned for himself than Jerusalem, since he had such a dreadful cup to drink, and was about to suffer such extreme things by the cruelty of Jerusalem that week. But he forgets his own sorrow and death and weeps over the misery of his cruel enemies. Pastors should imitate their Master in his fervent prayers for the good of the souls of men.

It was Jesus' manner, whenever he did anything special in his ministry, first to go alone and pour out his soul in extraordinary prayer to his Father. So, when he was about to go on a journey throughout Galilee to preach in their synagogues, *"he departed and went out to a desolate place, and there he prayed"* (Mark 1:35-39). When he was about to choose his twelve apostles and send them out to preach the gospel, he first went out into a mountain to pray, and continued all night in prayer to God (Luke 6:12). And the night before his crucifixion, where he offered himself as a sacrifice for our souls, he pours out his heart in extraordinary prayer for those he was about to die for (John 17).

That wonderful and most emotional prayer of his was not so much for himself as for his people. Although he knew what suffering he was to go through the next day, he almost seems to have had his heart filled with concern for his disciples. He shows this in spending so much time comforting and counseling them and praying for them with compassion, care, and fatherly tenderness. And the prayers that he made in the garden of Gethsemane, knowing the cup he was going to drink the next day, seem to be intercessory, especially the last of the three prayers he made when in an agony; he prayed more passionately, and his sweat was like great drops of blood falling to the ground. This was when he did not pray that the cup might pass from him, as he had done before, but that God's will might be done (Luke 22:44, Matt. 26:42).

That was a prayer he prayed as our High Priest (Heb. 5:6-7). Therefore, it must be a prayer of intercession for us, a prayer offered up with his blood which he sweated in his agony, as prayers were offered up with the blood of the sacrifices in the temple. His prayer at that time, *"Not my will, but yours, be done"* (Luke 22:42), was not only an expression of submission but had the form of a petition, as is in the Lord's prayer. He prayed that God's will might be done in his being enabled to do the will of God, persevering in obedience to death; and in the success of his sufferings, which might be called the will of God. *"Behold, I have come... I delight to do your will, O my God"* (Psalm 40:7-8).

Daily Reflections

As Christians, we should have a desire to see other people converted and born again. Part of that desire to see others come to know Jesus and have faith in him is to pray for them. But, often these prayers can be like our shopping lists —it is an item that we bring before God without much thought and even less compassion. To be moved as Jesus was when he saw the many people who were still lost without him would change the way we prayed for those around us. To have a real heart for the lost would see our prayers as persistent, desperate, and passionate.

1. Jesus regarded people's souls above his physical needs and honor. Can you say the same for yourself? Why?
2. What does compassion for others mean in this context? Do you naturally have compassion for others?
3. Have you ever prayed for a specific person or family member to become born again? What happened?
4. Does praying for the lost have anything to do with the Great Commission in Matthew 28:19-20?
5. Do you feel the kind of prayers that Jesus prayed are far out of reach from your own? Why?

24

EMOTIONAL PRAYER

"God is spirit, and those who worship him must worship in spirit and truth"
John 4:24

Some of us think that our prayers are real and true because of the religious emotions we have sometimes experienced. We may say that when we have come before God in prayer, we have not only used respectful terms and gestures, but we have prayed with emotion; our prayers have been with tears, which we think showed something in the heart. But these emotions have often come from other causes, and not from any true respect for God.

1. They have come from self-love, and not love for God.
   If you have cried before God because of your own

pitiful case, that has been because you loved yourself, and not because you had any respect for God. If your tears have been from sorrow for your sins, you have mourned for your sins, because you have sinned against yourself, and not because you have sinned against God. *"When you fasted and mourned in the fifth month and in the seventh, for these seventy years, was it for me that you fasted?"* (Zech. 7:5).

2. Pride and good thoughts about ourselves often have a great effect on the emotions of people. We have a good opinion of what we are doing when we are praying, and the reflection on that affects us—we are affected by our own goodness. Our self-righteousness often causes tears. A high opinion of ourselves before God, and an imagination of us having a good account with him, have affected us in our transactions with God. There is often an abundance of pride in the midst of tears, and often pride is the source of them. And then we are so far from thinking that we are not an enemy to God that on the contrary, we are. In your tears, you are, in a vain conceit of yourself, exalting yourself against God.

The emotions of people often come from the wrong notions we have of God. We think of God the way we do with other people, as though he is able to be moved by his emotions. We see him as one whose heart can be drawn, whose emotions can be moved by what he sees in us. We conceive of him as being swayed by our performance, and this stirs up our emotions. So, one tear brings another, and our emotions increase by reflection. And often we think of God as someone that loves us, and is a friend to us, and this plays on our affections. But such emotions that rise to God, in the picture we see of him, do not mean that we might not have any hatred toward God when we see him for who he really is.

Saul was moved by his feelings when David confronted him about pursuing him and seeking to kill him. David's words played on Saul's affections. *"As soon as David had finished speaking these words to Saul, Saul said, 'Is this your voice, my son David?' And Saul lifted up his voice and wept"* (1 Sam. 24:16). He was so affected that he wept aloud and called David his son, though moments before, he wanted to kill him. But this emotion of Saul did not mean that he would stop his hatred for David. He was David's mortal enemy before and sought his life, and so he did afterward. It was just an ache in his feelings—his hatred was not done away with. The next news we hear of Saul is that he was pursuing David and seeking his life again. We cannot think that people are not enemies because we are affected and shed tears in our prayers.

Daily Reflections

We are emotional people—God made humans to be emotional. But, many times, this overrides any logical thought or process and we end up acting in anger or sympathy when we should have rather held back. However, there is something else we should be led by when it comes to our spiritual walk with the Lord: not emotions or logic, but the Spirit. We are often moved in our prayers and overcome by our emotions as we push into something close to our 'hearts.' We need to make sure that this is in line with God's will and the Holy Spirit's guidance so that we are not swept up in feelings.

1. Are you naturally an emotional or a logical person? Does this affect the way you pray?
2. Do you think emotion in prayer is a good or a bad thing? Why?
3. The Bible is full of emotions, even when it comes to God being angry or Jesus weeping for other people. Is it possible to be emotional and in the Spirit?
4. Why are we so often led astray by what we feel rather than hearing God's voice?
5. Have you ever thought that pride can be a strong emotion that dictates the way we act?

25

PRAYING FOR GOD'S WILL IN SUFFERING

"My Father, if this cannot pass unless I drink it, your will be done"
Matthew 26:42

What did Jesus seek for in this prayer? That God's will might be done in his suffering.

"The will of the Lord be done" is sometimes understood as a request, as in the Lord's prayer, *"Your will be done, on earth as it is in heaven"* (Matt. 6:10). There the words are understood both as an expression of submission, and also a request. Jesus spoke the same words at the end of his first prayer, *"Nevertheless, not my will, but yours, be done"* (Luke 22:42). So, what he was wrestling with God about in this prayer was that God's will might be done in relation to his suffering.

This implies a request that he might be strengthened and supported and enabled to do God's will by going through these sufferings. This is the same as when he says, *"Behold, I have come to do your will, O God, as it is written of me in the scroll of the book"* (Heb. 10:7). It was the preceptive will of God that he should take that cup and drink it. It was the Father's command for him. This was the greatest act of obedience that Jesus was to perform. He prays for strength and help that his poor weak human nature might be supported, that he might not fail in this great trial, that he might not sink and be swallowed up, and his strength overcome that he should not endure, and finish the appointed obedience.

This was the thing that he feared and is spoken of in Hebrews 5:7 when he says, *"he was heard because of his reverence."* When he was fully aware of the terrible sufferings, it amazed him. He was afraid that his poor, weak strength should be overcome, and that he should fail in such a great trial, that he should be swallowed up by the death that he was to die, and so should not be saved from death. Therefore, he cried with tears to him that was able to strengthen, support, and save him from death, that the death he was to suffer might not overcome his love and obedience, but that he might overcome death, and be saved from it.

If Jesus' courage had failed in the trial, and he had not endured his suffering, he never would have been saved from death but would have sunk in the deep mire. He never would have risen from the dead because his rising from the dead was a reward for his victory. If his courage had failed, and he had given up, he would have remained under the power of death, and we would all have perished—we would have remained in our sins. If he had failed, all would have failed. If he had not overcome in that trial, we could not have been freed from death, we would all have perished together.

Therefore, this was the saving from death that the apostle speaks of, that Christ feared and prayed for with strong crying and tears. His being overcome by death was the thing that he feared, and so he was heard in that he feared. This Jesus prayed, that the will of God might be done in his sufferings, that he might not disobey God's will in his sufferings. So, it follows in the next verse in that passage of Hebrews 5:8, *"Although he was a son, he learned obedience through what he suffered."* Jesus, in his agony, prayed that the will of God might be done—that he might have the strength to do his will, and might not sink and fail in such great sufferings.

This is confirmed in the psalms where we see a representation of Jesus' prayer to God when his soul was overwhelmed with sorrow: *"Save me, O God! For the waters have come up to my neck. I sink in deep mire, where there is no foothold; I have come into deep waters, and the flood sweeps over me"* (Psalm 69:1-2). But then what is represented as the thing he feared, was failing and being overwhelmed in this great trial. *"Deliver me from sinking in the mire; let me be delivered from my enemies and from the deep waters. Let not the flood sweep over me, or the deep swallow me up, or the pit close its mouth over me"* (Psalm 69:14-15). *"But you, O LORD, do not be far off! O you my help, come quickly to my aid! Deliver my soul from the sword, my precious life from the power of the dog! Save me from the mouth of the lion!"* (Psalm 22:19-21). It was acceptable that Jesus should seek help from God to enable him to do his will because he needed God's help. After all, his human nature, without divine help, was not strong enough to carry him through.

Daily Reflections

What is God's will? That is a question we all ask, and we all want the answer to. Jesus does not ask that question, though; he is clear in what was being asked of him. His prayer was that he would be able to fulfill his mandate. Sometimes we spend so much time trying to find God's will instead of asking for the strength to do what is clearly laid out for us as his will in the Scriptures. Jesus knew that his human strength was not able to sustain him, and he knew that only his Father could supernaturally see him through the last few hours of life. We need the same!

1. What do you think God's will is for your life?
2. Read Luke 9:23. Does this have any bearing on God's will and what we need to face in fulfilling it?
3. What is your view on suffering in your life? Is it something to try and pray away or to embrace and see that God is glorified in it?
4. What do you understand by Hebrews 5:8, "he learned obedience through what he suffered," for your own life?
5. How does submission play a role in God's will and enduring suffering for his glory?

26

PRAYING FOR IMPORTANT BLESSINGS

"They ought always to pray and not lose heart"
Luke 18:1

We should not pray to God in a cold and careless manner, but with sincerity of spirit, especially when we are praying for things that are important, such as spiritual and eternal blessings. When we go before God with a cold, dull heart and in a lifeless manner pray for eternal blessings that are important to our souls, we should think of Jesus' prayers that he poured out to God, with tears and bloody sweat. Thinking about this might make us ashamed of our dull, lifeless prayers that are more denial than asking to be heard. The language of our praying does not see the importance of what we are praying for; we are indifferent to whether God answers us or not.

The example of Jacob wrestling with God for the blessing should teach us sincerity and perseverance in our prayers, but more especially the example of Jesus, who wrestled with God in a bloody sweat. If we were aware, as Jesus was, of the great importance of those blessings that are of eternal consequence, our prayers would be different than they are now. Our souls would be engaged in this duty with more effort.

There are many blessings that we ask God for in our prayers, which are as important to us as those which Jesus asked God for in his agony. It is just as important that we are enabled to do the will of God, and can have persevering obedience to his commands, as it was to Jesus that he should not fail to do God's will. It is as important to us to be saved from death, as it was to Jesus that he should have victory over death and be saved from it. It is as important to us, that Jesus' redemption should be successful in us, as it was to him that God's will should be done, in the fruits and success of his redemption.

Jesus recommended sincere vigilance and being in prayer to his disciples, through his prayer and example to them. When he was in agony and found his disciples asleep, he asked them to watch and pray *"Watch and pray that you may not enter into temptation. The spirit indeed is willing, but the flesh is weak"* (Matt. 26:41). At the same time, he set them an example of what he had commanded them— while they slept, he watched and poured out his soul in those sincere prayers that you have heard of. In other places, he taught us to ask for those blessings of God that are very important, as people who will not be denied. We have another example of the great conflicts between Jesus' spirit and his participation in this duty. *"In these days he went out to the mountain to pray, and all night he continued in prayer to God"* (Luke 6:12).

He often recommended perseverance to God in prayers, such as in the parable of the unjust judge:

And he told them a parable to the effect that they ought always to pray and not lose heart. He said, "In a certain city there was a judge who neither feared God nor respected man. And there was a widow in that city who kept coming to him and saying, 'Give me justice against my adversary.' For a while he refused, but afterward he said to himself, 'Though I neither fear God nor respect man, yet because this widow keeps bothering me, I will give her justice, so that she will not beat me down by her continual coming.'" And the Lord said, "Hear what the unrighteous judge says." (Luke 18:1-6)

And the persistent friend:

And he said to them, "Which of you who has a friend will go to him at midnight and say to him, 'Friend, lend me three loaves, for a friend of mine has arrived on a journey, and I have nothing to set before him'; and he will answer from within, 'Do not bother me; the door is now shut, and my children are with me in bed. I cannot get up and give you anything'? I tell you, though he will not get up and give him anything because he is his friend, yet because of his impudence he will rise and give him whatever he needs." (Luke 11:5-8)

He also taught about answering prayer, when he answered the woman of Canaan:

And behold, a Canaanite woman from that region came out and was crying, "Have mercy on me, O Lord, Son of David; my daughter is severely oppressed by a demon." But he did not answer her a word.

And his disciples came and begged him, saying, "Send her away, for she is crying out after us." He answered, "I was sent only to the lost sheep of the house of Israel." But she came and knelt before him, saying, "Lord, help me." And he answered, "It is not right to take the children's bread and throw it to the dogs." She said, "Yes, Lord, yet even the dogs eat the crumbs that fall from their masters' table." Then Jesus answered her, "O woman, great is your faith! Be it done for you as you desire." And her daughter was healed instantly. (Matt. 15:22-28)

Daily Reflections

We love praying for blessings. Who doesn't? It means we ask for something good and we get something great in return. But often our concept of what blessings are important to our lives ends up being material, physical things that make us more comfortable in the end. Jesus' view of what was important was always linked to his Father and what would bring him glory. Although God will not deny us the things we need, our view of what is significant to him needs to change if we are to start praying for those blessings that he wants to give us.

1. Why are vigilance and determination such key factors when Edwards is speaking about important blessings?
2. Can you identify with the persistent widow and the friend who asks for bread or not? Why?
3. Why does God not give blessings of an eternal consequence to us lightly? Why does he want us to wrestle for them?

4. What do you think of Jesus' answer to the Canaanite woman? Was it not a bit too harsh?
5. Do you have the faith to persevere in prayer for important blessings?

27

PRAYERS OF THE SAINTS

"And the smoke of the incense, with the prayers of the saints,
rose before God from the hand of the angel"
Revelation 8:4

God respects the prayers of Christians in his handling of the affairs of the world. We can see this in the representation made at the beginning of Revelation 8. There we read of seven angels standing before the throne of God, receiving seven trumpets from him, that when they were blown, great and mighty changes would happen in the world. But when these angels had received their trumpets, they must stand still, and all must be silent; not one of them must be allowed to make a sound until the prayers of the saints are heard and answered.

The angel of the covenant, as a glorious high priest, comes and stands at the altar, with incense to offer the prayers of all saints on the golden altar before the throne. The smoke of the incense, with these prayers of the saints, ascends with acceptance before God, out of the angel's hand—then the angels will prepare themselves to sound their instruments. And God, in the events of every trumpet, remembers those prayers. This is seen in the great and glorious things he accomplishes for his church in answer to these prayers, in the event of the last trumpet, which brings the glory of the last days when these prayers shall be turned into joyful praises. *"Then the seventh angel blew his trumpet, and there were loud voices in heaven, saying, 'The kingdom of the world has become the kingdom of our Lord and of his Christ, and he shall reign forever and ever.' And the twenty-four elders who sit on their thrones before God fell on their faces and worshiped God, saying, 'We give thanks to you, Lord God Almighty, who is and who was, for you have taken your great power and begun to reign'"* (Rev. 11:15-17).

Why Does God Honor Our Prayers?

Since it is God's pleasure to honor his people, to perform the works of his kingdom in this way—by the prayers of his saints—then we can assume that whenever the time comes, God gives an extraordinary spirit of prayer for the fulfillment of his kingdom on earth which is his main goal, and the thing that the spirit of prayer in the saints aims for: God's kingdom to come.

God, in his grace, is pleased to show himself at the command of his people with regard to these blessings, to be ready to give them whenever we shall pray for them. *"Thus says the Lord, the Holy One of Israel, and the one who formed him: 'Ask me of things to come; will you command me concerning my children and the work of my hands?'"* (Isa. 45:11). What God is speaking of, in this context, is the restoration of his church— not only a restoration from physical disaster but also a spiritual restoration and fulfillment by God commanding the heavens to *"let the clouds rain down righteousness; let the earth open, that salvation and righteousness may bear fruit"* (Isa. 45:8).

God wants his people to ask him, or inquire by sincere prayer, to do this for them. He shows himself to be at the command of sincere prayers for such a blessing. The reason why he is so ready to hear such prayers is because it is prayer for his own church, his chosen and beloved people, his children, and the work of his hands. God stands ready to be gracious to his church, to appear for its restoration, and is waiting to hear the cries of his people for it, that he may answer their prayers. *"Therefore the Lord waits to be gracious to you, and therefore he exalts himself to show mercy to you. For the Lord is a God of justice; blessed are all those who wait for him. For a people shall dwell in Zion, in Jerusalem; you shall weep no more. He will surely be gracious to you at the sound of your cry. As soon as he hears it, he answers you"* (Isa. 30:18-19). These words imply that when God sees his people praying for this blessing, it will not be delayed.

Daily Reflections

To be called a saint sounds strange, and yet that is what we are. All through the Bible, it talks about those who have faith in God, those who keep his commands and follow his ways, as the saints. We use the more popular term Christian, which simply means a follower of Christ. Saint has a more holy and pious ring to it, but that is what we are: a holy people and a royal priesthood. It is no wonder that God esteems the prayers of this kind of people as holy and acceptable.

1. Do you see yourself as a saint, a holy person, and a child of God?
2. Why do you think the angels must first wait until our prayers are heard and answered?
3. Why do you think our prayers are called incense that rises to God? See Psalm 141:2.
4. What is the relation between the prayers of the saints and God's kingdom that is coming?
5. Why is God so ready to hear our prayers in this regard?

28

IRREVERENCE IN PRAYER

"For although they knew God, they did not honor him as God or give thanks to him, but they became futile in their thinking, and their foolish hearts were darkened"
Romans 1:21

By following God's commands, yet living in sin, we show great irreverence and contempt for those holy practices. When we commit sin, live in it, and attend sacred worship and rituals of God, and then go from church directly to carry on sinning, we show a very irreverent spirit for holy things and have contempt for God's sacred customs.

We show that we have no reverence for the God who has made those practices holy. We show contempt for that divine authority that instituted them. We show an irreverent spirit toward the God into whose presence we come, and in whose name these practices are performed. We show contempt for the adoration of God, of faith and love, humility, submission, and praise, which prayer and worship were made to express. What an irreverent spirit it shows when we are so careless about how we come before God! We do not take time to cleanse and purify ourselves to be ready to come before God! We do not avoid making ourselves even more unclean and filthy!

We have often been taught that God is too pure to look at our sins and is offended by them. Yet we do not care how unclean and abominable we come into his presence. It shows terrible irreverence and contempt that we are so bold, that we are not afraid to come into God's presence in such a manner. We will presume to go out of his presence, and from praying and worshiping, to carry on in our sinful ways. If we had any reverence for God and holy things, approaching his presence, and performing those holy practices, we would not dare to go from them into sin.

It would show a great irreverence in any person toward a king if we should not care how we came into his presence, and if we should come in a wretched habit, and a very indecent manner. How much more irreverence does it show, for people who willingly defile themselves with that filth which God infinitely hates, and so frequently come into the presence of God in this way!

By pretending to show respect for prayer and worship, and then acting in another way in our lives, we mock God. By joining in prayer, in public worship, confessions, petitions, and thanksgivings, we make a show of righteousness before God, and of humbling ourselves before him; of sorrow for our sins, thankfulness for blessings, and a desire for grace and help to obey and serve God. By listening to the preaching, we make a show of having a teachable spirit, and being ready to practice all the instructions we have heard. By sharing in communion, we make a show of faith in Christ, choosing him for our portion, and spiritually feeding on him.

But by our actions, we declare the contrary. We declare that we have no high esteem for God, but that we despise him in our hearts. We declare that we are so far from repenting and that we intend to continue in our sins. We declare that we have no desire for that grace and assistance to live in the holy way we prayed for and that we would rather live sinfully. This is what we choose.

When we perform holy duties, and yet willingly live in sin, we treat Christ in the same manner that the Jews did when they mocked him on the cross. We come to public worship, pretend to pray to him, sing his praises, sit and hear his word, and take communion, pretending to commemorate his death. So, we kneel before him, and say, *"Hail, King of the Jews!"* (John 19:3) yet at the same time, we live in sin, which we know Jesus has forbidden, hates, and dishonors him. So, we strike him and spit in his face. We do the same as Judas did, who came to Christ saying, *"Hail, Master"* (Matt. 26:49 KJV), and kissed him, at the same time betraying him into the hands of those who wanted to kill him.

Daily Reflections

The fear of God, or reverence as we have come to know it these days, is critical in the manner that we approach the throne room of the Almighty. It is an accepted part of prayer and worship, almost so much that we take it for granted sometimes and, without knowing it, actually come to him in a way that is anything but respectful, filled with awe and worship, or submissive. Irreverence creeps in when we simply fulfill our duties and have very little heart for what we are actually doing. God hates this, calls it hypocritical, and would rather we did not come to him at all.

1. This is another of Edwards' passages that come across as harsh. Do you find the tone easy to accept or more like a rebuke? Why?
2. Have you ever come to God irreverently? Why?
3. Why is sin such an integral part of having a lack of the fear of God?
4. Read Hebrews 10:26-31 in connection with what Edwards says here. What do you understand by these verses?
5. What does it mean to pray with the fear of the Lord?

29

JESUS, OUR MEDIATOR

"For there is one God, and there is one mediator between God and men,
the man Christ Jesus"
1 Timothy 2:5

There are three spiritual beings: the Father, Son, and Holy Spirit. Jesus was a suitable person for a redeemer. It was not right that the redeemer should be God the Father because he, in the working of Trinity, was the person who holds the rights of the Godhead, and so was the person offended, whose justice required satisfaction—he was to be appeased by a mediator. It was not right it should be the Holy Spirit because the mediator is between the Father and believers, and is between the Father and the Spirit. Christians, in all their spiritual transactions with God, act by the

Spirit: it is the Spirit of God that acts in us; we are the temples of the Holy Spirit. The Holy Spirit dwelling in us, is their principle of action, in all our transactions with God.

But in our spiritual transactions with God, we act by a mediator. These spiritual and holy practices cannot be acceptable, or have any success with God, as from a fallen creature, but by a mediator. Therefore, Jesus, in being the mediator between the Father and Christians, can be said to be a mediator between the Father and the Holy Spirit that acts in us.

And therefore it was right that the mediator should not be the Father or the Spirit, but a middle person between them both. It is the Spirit in us that seeks the blessing of God, by faith and prayer; and, as the apostle says, with groanings that cannot be uttered. *"Likewise the Spirit helps us in our weakness. For we do not know what to pray for as we ought, but the Spirit himself intercedes for us with groanings too deep for words"* (Rom. 8:26). The Spirit in us seeks divine blessings from God by and through a mediator; and therefore that mediator must not be the Spirit, but another person.

The doctrine of perseverance is shown in the nature of the mediation of Jesus. Because he is a mediator to reconcile God to man and man to God, and as he is a middle person between both, and has the nature of both, so he undertakes for each and becomes a guarantee for each with the other. He undertakes and becomes a guarantee for man to God. He engages for him, that the law that was given will be answered, that justice will be satisfied, and the honor of God's majesty vindicated.

So he undertakes and engages for the Father with us, in order for us to be reconciled to God, and persuaded to come to him, to love him, trust confidently in him, and rest quietly in him. He undertakes for the Father's acceptance and favor, *"And he who loves me will be loved by my Father"* (John 14:21). He ensures that the Father shall hear and answer our prayers. He becomes a guarantee to see that our prayers are answered; *"Whatever you ask in my name, this I will do, that the Father may be glorified in the Son"* (John 14:13). He ensures that we will have the necessary grace from the Father.

It was necessary that someone should undertake for God with people, for his forgiveness and sanctifying grace, in order for sinners to be fully reconciled to God. Jesus is in a capacity to undertake for us, and be a guarantee for us, with the Father, because he puts himself in our place—the Father has put him there as a priest who answers for us, and suffers what we should have suffered, and as a king.

He is appointed to govern the world, so he answers for God to us, and gives us what we need from God. He undertakes for us in things that are expected of us as subjects, because he appears in the form of a servant for us. So, he undertakes for the Father, in that which is desired and hoped for of him as king—the Father has put him into his kingdom and dominion and has given all authority and power to him.

Daily Reflections

This is a crucial aspect of understanding the workings of prayer, and Edwards does a wonderful job of explaining the godhead and each person's responsibility when it comes to our worship and prayer. When we can truly understand the role of a mediator in relation to the Father, the Spirit, and us, then we can appreciate the sacrifice and the importance Jesus plays in our prayers. Without him, there would be no way that God would even listen to our sinful mutterings.

1. In your own words, what is Jesus' role as a mediator? Why is this necessary?
2. Look at Hebrews 9:15. How does this fit in with your definition?
3. Why is the notion of a guarantee so important when it comes to Jesus being a mediator?
4. We know John 14:6 well, where it says that there is no other way but through Jesus. What do you make of people who pray to or through other people and saints? Are those also mediators?
5. Compare this with the key verse in 1 Timothy 2:5.

30

JESUS' PRAYER FOR THE HOLY SPIRIT TO COME

"And I will ask the Father, and he will give you another Helper,
to be with you forever, even the Spirit of truth"
John 14:16-17

The sum of the blessings Jesus sought, by what he did and suffered in the work of redemption, was the Holy Spirit.

This is our redemption: The Father provides and gives the Redeemer, and the price of redemption is offered to him, and he grants the benefit purchased. The Son is the Redeemer who gives the price and also is the price offered. The Holy Spirit is the grand blessing obtained by the price offered, and given to those who are redeemed.

The Holy Spirit, living in us, his influences and fruits, is the sum of all grace, holiness, comfort, and joy. It is the spiritual good Jesus purchased for people in this world. It is also the sum of all perfection, glory, and eternal joy, that he purchased for them in the world still to come. The Holy Spirit is the subject of the promises, both of the eternal covenant of redemption, and also of the covenant of grace.

This is the grand subject of the promises of the Old Testament, so often recorded in the prophecies of the Messiah's kingdom. It is the main subject of the promises of the New Testament, particularly of the covenant of grace delivered by Jesus Christ to his disciples, as his last will and testament, in the 14th, 15th, and 16th chapters of John. The grand legacy that he gave to them, in his last discussion with them. Therefore, the Holy Spirit is so often called the Spirit of promise, and emphatically, the promise, the promise of the Father.

Since this is the great blessing Jesus purchased for us by his work and sufferings on earth, it was what he received from the Father when he went up into heaven and entered into the holy of holies with his own blood, that he might give it to those whom he had redeemed. *"It is to your advantage that I go away, for if I do not go away, the Helper will not come to you. But if I go, I will send him to you"* (John 16:7). *"Being therefore exalted at the right hand of God, and having received from the Father the promise of the Holy Spirit, he has poured out this that you yourselves are seeing and hearing"* (Acts 2:33).

This is the sum of those gifts, which Jesus received for us, even for the rebellious, at his ascension. These are the benefits he obtained for us by his intercession; *"And I will ask the*

Father, and he will give you another Helper, to be with you forever, even the Spirit of truth." This is Jesus' fullness, even in his being full of the Spirit; he was so full of grace and truth, that we might receive this fullness, and grace for grace. He is anointed with the Holy Spirit, and this is the ointment that goes down from the head to the rest of the members in the body, which is us. *"He gives the Spirit without measure* [to him, and to] *each one of us according to the measure of Christ's gift"* (John 3:34; Eph. 4:7).

This, therefore, was the great blessing he prayed for in that wonderful prayer which he said for his disciples and all the church the evening before he died, recorded in John 17. The blessing he prayed for to the Father, on behalf of his disciples, was the same he had insisted on in his discussion with them before; and this was the same blessing he prayed for, when, as our High Priest, he cried with tears and blood (Heb. 5:6-7). It was for this that he shed his blood; for this, he also shed tears and poured out prayers.

Daily Reflections

Without the Holy Spirit, we would be lost in our prayers and be struggling through our useless words to communicate things in the spirit. It is why Jesus knew it was so important to ensure that we would receive the Comforter as our guide and help. In his last prayer for the disciples, he prayed as he did for us, that the Spirit would come and assist us, that we would be able to speak, think, and hear spiritually, and that we would know the will of God for our lives.

Jesus' Prayer for the Holy Spirit to Come | 123

1. Why does Edwards see the Holy Spirit as the greatest blessing that we can receive?
2. Why is the Holy Spirit so important when it comes to our prayers?
3. Do you pray in and with the Spirit? If you do, how do you know?
4. Read Romans 8:26-27. What is the significance of this verse for us?
5. Is there a difference between receiving the Holy Spirit, the Spirit falling on you, and being baptized in the Spirit?

31

AN EXAMPLE TO WATCH AND PRAY

"But stay awake at all times, praying that you may have strength to escape all these things that are going to take place, and to stand before the Son of Man"
Luke 21:36

The cross was to Jesus the way to the crown of glory, and so it is to his disciples. His behavior, under those circumstances, was a good example for them to follow. They should observe after what manner he entered into the kingdom of heaven and obtained the crown of glory, and so they also should run the race that is set before them. *"Therefore, since we are surrounded by so great a cloud of witnesses, let us also lay aside every weight, and sin which clings so closely, and let us run with endurance the race that is set before us, looking to Jesus, the founder and perfecter of our faith, who for the joy that was set before*

An Example to Watch and Pray | 125

him endured the cross, despising the shame, and is seated at the right hand of the throne of God" (Heb. 12:1-2).

1. When others are asleep, we should be awake, as it was with Jesus. The time of his agony was at night, the time when people are usually asleep. It was the time when the disciples who were with Jesus were asleep, but he had something else to do rather than to sleep—he stayed awake, with his heart engaged in this work. So it should be with believers, that when the souls of our neighbors are asleep in their sins, lethargic and unaware, we should watch and pray, and maintain an active awareness of the importance of our spiritual concerns. *"So then let us not sleep, as others do, but let us keep awake and be sober"* (1 Thess. 5:6).

2. We should do our duties with determination, as Jesus did. The time when others were asleep was a time when Jesus was busy, and was engaged with all his strength, agonizing in it, struggling and wrestling in tears and blood. So, we should use our time to be engaged in this work, pushing through the opposition we meet with, pushing through all difficulties and sufferings in the way, running the race set before us with patience, struggling with the enemies of our souls with all our strength, as those who wrestle not with flesh and blood but with principalities and powers, and the rulers of the darkness of this world, and spiritual wickedness in high places.

126 | JONATHAN EDWARDS ON PRAYER

3. This striving should be so that God may be glorified, and our own eternal happiness is obtained by doing God's will. It was the same with Jesus: What he strived for was to do the will of God, that he might keep his command, and in this way, God's will might be done, and salvation would be obtained by his sufferings. Here is an example for us to follow: We should strive to do the will of our heavenly Father, so that we may *"discern what is the will of God, what is good and acceptable and perfect"* (Rom. 12:2) and glorify God.

4. In all we have to do, our eyes should be on God for his help to enable us to overcome. Jesus did not overcome by his own strength, but his eyes were on God. He cried to him for help and strength to uphold him that he might not fail. He watched and prayed, as he wanted his disciples to do. He wrestled with his enemies and with his great sufferings, but at the same time wrestled with God to obtain his help, to enable him to get the victory. So, Christians should not depend on their own strength but cry to God for his strength to make them conquerors.

5. In this way, we should hold out to the end as Jesus did. Jesus was successful, obtained the victory, and won the prize. He overcame and sat down with the Father on his throne. So, Christians should persevere and hold out to the end; they should continue to run their race until they have reached the end. They should be faithful to death as Jesus was. Then, when they have overcome, they will sit down with him on his throne. *"The one who conquers, I will grant him to sit*

with me on my throne, as I also conquered and sat down with my Father on his throne" (Rev. 3:21).

Daily Reflections

Jesus is our best and ultimate example in everything for Christianity, especially when it comes to praying. There is no one else who can easily match him for his determination and his passion when it comes to speaking to the Father. His last prayer in the Garden of Gethsemane is perhaps the most clear and vivid instance of how we should approach God. But too often we are like the disciples, our spirits are very willing to press in, but our flesh is incredibly weak and resistant to watch and pray.

1. Do you find it easy to pray when others are 'asleep' and not praying at all?
2. What does it mean to be alert in prayer?
3. Why do you think it is important that we strive in our prayers?
4. Why is it important that we do not try this in our own strength, but we keep our eyes on God as our help?
5. Why is the picture of running a race, as in the key verse, such a good portrayal of our Christian journey in prayer?

IF YOU ENJOYED this book and would like to read another one just like it, you can find more insights by classic Christian authors in a 31-day format:

- E.M. Bounds Prayer: *31 Life-Changing Insights from E.M. Bounds on How to Pray with Daily Reflections*
- J.C. Ryle on Prayer: *31 Insights for Understanding the Purpose and Power of Prayer*
- C.H. Spurgeon on Prayer: *31 Effective Insights on How to Pray with Daily Reflections*
- John Bunyan on Prayer: *31 Biblical Insights for Effective Prayer*

ABOUT JONATHAN EDWARDS

Jonathan Edwards was born on October 5, 1703 in Connecticut. He was the only son of a low-income minister. Despite this, he received an excellent education, helped by his father and elder sisters. At 13, he entered Yale College and followed his deep interest in science. He kept a notebook where he wrote much about spiders and atomic theory.

Even after studying theology, he reverted to his love for science, seeing God's creation as a masterful scientific design. Edwards filled the position of a lay preacher at a Presbyterian church but did not take up their offer to stay on, instead becoming a rector at Yale until 1726.

A year later, he was ordained and took up the position of assisting his grandfather, Solomon Stoddard. He married Sarah Pierpont, who would go on to bear him 11 children. When his grandfather passed away two years later, Edwards took over what was then the largest and wealthiest congregation of that colony.

In the early 1730s, a revival broke out, known as the First Great Awakening, that would shake the region and allow Edwards to study one of his long-time fascinations: conversion. His fame spread and he became good friends with George Whitefield, who was traveling the region at that time.

In 1741, revival sprang up again, and it was here that Edwards preached his most famous sermon, *Sinners in the Hands of an Angry God*. Rather than an angry rebuke, Edwards' quiet, contemplative style of preaching was a more methodical encouragement to turn to God.

He fell out with his congregation and was dismissed, seeing disparities in the beliefs on communion and baptism. The dispute became bitter to the point that he was rejected by his own council. However, he continued to preach to Mohicans in the region and to others. His preaching was not accepted by his own church, as they saw his style and doctrine as unpopular. In greater New England, Edwards' writing and sermons were still in high demand.

Edwards continued his attack on false beliefs surrounding communion, with a few of his letters as responses to certain people who publicly tried to oppose him.

He finally moved to Massachusetts after declining offers in Scotland and Virginia, where he became pastor of a small church and a missionary to the local American Indians. In 1758, he became president of the College of New Jersey, and in a drive to encourage vaccines against smallpox, he was inoculated. He did not survive the effects, though, and died shortly after on March 22.

His clear Calvinistic, Puritan beliefs gave the churches a strong doctrinal path to follow. Leaving behind copious written work and sermons, his ideas and careful considerations have become timeless signposts for many Christians and ministers hundreds of years after his death.

He also penned *The Life of David Brainerd,* a biographical account that inspired many other missionaries for years to come.

BIBLIOGRAPHY

Crossway. (2001). *English Standard Version Bible*. Crossway Bibles.

Digital Puritan Press. (n.d.). *Jonathan Edwards*. Digitalpuritan.net. http://digitalpuritan.net/jonathan-edwards/

Thomas Nelson Publishers. (2014). *Holy Bible, Kjv*. Thomas Nelson Pub.

www.ingramcontent.com/pod-product-compliance
Lightning Source LLC
LaVergne TN
LVHW020437070526
838199LV00063B/4764